# AUTOCRATS AND ACADEMICS

# AUTOCRATS AND ACADEMICS

*Education, Culture, and Society*

*in Tsarist Russia*

JAMES C. McCLELLAND

THE UNIVERSITY OF CHICAGO PRESS
*Chicago & London*

THE UNIVERSITY OF CHICAGO PRESS, CHICAGO 60637
THE UNIVERSITY OF CHICAGO PRESS, LTD., LONDON
© 1979 by The University of Chicago
All rights reserved. Published 1979
Printed in the United States of America
86 85 84 83 82 81 80 79      1 2 3 4 5

JAMES C. MCCLELLAND is associate professor of history
at the University of Nebraska, Lincoln.

Library of Congress Cataloging in Publication Data

McClelland, James C
    Autocrats and academics, education, culture, and
society in Tsarist Russia.

    Bibliography: p.
    Includes index.
    1. Education—Russia—History.   2. Russia—
Intellectual life—1801-1917.   3. Student movements—
Russia.   I. Title.
LA831.8.M24        370'.947        79-12504
ISBN 0-226-55661-1

# CONTENTS

# CONTENTS

# TABLES

# ACKNOWLEDGMENTS

IT IS A GREAT PLEASURE TO EXPRESS MY WARM APPRECIATION FOR THE assistance, advice, and support I have received from a number of individuals and institutions while working on this project. My greatest debt is to Alexander Vucinich, who in the course of many conversations generously shared his unparalleled knowledge of Russian science, education, and society. Those who were kind enough to read all or part of the manuscript include Reginald E. Zelnik, S. Frederick Starr, William G. Rosenberg, Christine Johanson, James Cobb Mills, Terence Emmons, Lawrence Badash, and Daniel R. Brower. Many of their comments were invaluable in helping to improve the final version, but since I did not always take their advice, they bear no responsibility for inadequacies that remain. C. Warren Hollister made, at a critical juncture, an important suggestion without which this book might not have appeared in its present form. John Haley served as both a skilled research assistant and a helpful critic. The University of California at Santa Barbara and the American Council of Learned Societies provided grants which greatly facilitated the research and writing. Special thanks are due to Arlene Paul, now retired, and the entire library staff of the Hoover Institution on War, Revolution, and Peace, who always helped to make my time there pleasant as well as productive. Alexandra Filippenko, Slavic Librarian at the University of California at Santa Barbara, was extremely cooperative in helping me locate and obtain necessary research material. Virginia Gibson typed the many drafts of the manuscript with skill, speed, and good humor.

The book is gratefully dedicated to the inspiring memory of my mother and to my father for his continuing loyal support.

J.C.M.

# INTRODUCTION

My own Sweetheart,
   Tho' I am very tired I must begin my letter this evening, so as
not to forget what our Friend told me. I gave yr. message & He
sends His love & says not to worry, all will be right. . . . Now
Sturmer wants to propose this Pr. Obolensky. . . to become
minister of the Interior, but Gregory begs you earnestly to
name Protopopov there. . . .[1]

SO WROTE EMPRESS ALEXANDRA TO HER HUSBAND IN SEPTEMBER 1916.
After a feeble effort at resistance, Nicholas consented. Appointments to
the highest positions in the Russian government at this desperate time
were indeed being influenced by "our Friend," the illiterate and de-
bauched Gregory Rasputin.
   Rasputin's rise to prominence at court can well be taken as symbolic
of one side of prerevolutionary Russia — a country where four out of five
inhabitants were peasants and two out of three illiterate; a nation which
found itself engaged in a war against a far more advanced enemy, and
ruled by a royal couple whose values and outlook were hopelessly
anachronistic. This backwardness was undoubtedly a major cause of her
collapse in World War I. But Russia's history before the war, much less
the nature of the two revolutions of 1917, can hardly be understood if
one ignores the fact that side by side with its traditional backwardness,
the tsarist empire also exhibited an exciting dynamism. For it was
"backward" Russia that produced the ballet of Fokine and Diaghilev
and the music of Stravinsky which shocked Parisian audiences before
the war. It was "backward" Russia that produced a Mendeleev, a
Pavlov, and enrolled more students in higher educational institutions
than any other country in the world except the United States. And it was
"backward" Russia that experienced during the 1890s one of the fastest
industrial growth rates of any country in the world, along with most of
the social tensions that the early stages of industrialization entail. Russia
on the eve of revoution was neither completely backward nor uniformly

modern, but a land of striking contrasts and forceful currents of change.

What were the causes of this strange mixture of innovation and tradition, of rapid change and stultifying stagnation? To what extent did this condition flow naturally and perhaps inevitably from such uncontrollable factors as Russia's vast size, remote geographical location, and long-standing autocratic tradition — factors dictating that *any* effort to modernize would result in unusually large rifts and divisions in the social fabric? How great a role, on the other hand, did the deliberately chosen reform policies of the tsars plus the prevailing attitudes and activities of the informed public play in either mitigating or exacerbating these contrasts? Can we, in short, distinguish and assess the relative impact of specific decisions and clearly traceable beliefs as opposed to impersonal forces and the dead weight of tradition in contributing to the development of the huge social and cultural contrasts of late Imperial Russia?

An analysis of the implementation and development of a formal educational system in Russia is a particularly fruitful way to approach this problem. The nature and unequal distribution of education in Russia was not the only factor which served as both cause and reflection of the schisms in the population; one could also point to the maldistribution of wealth, the lingering impact of serfdom and traditional patterns of social stratification, or the continuing weakness of administrative links between the center and the localities. But the specific contours of Russian education, much more than the nature of these other problems, were the direct product of conscious, deliberate policies, policies which were often debated at the highest levels of both government and society. Russia's size and poverty, to be sure, did dictate important limitations on the type of educational system that could be developed, but on the whole one is impressed primarily by the relatively wide freedom of choice open to educational planners and reformers.

As early as the seventeenth century certain political and religious leaders began to perceive potential advantages for Russian security and development in a systematic dissemination of technical and intellectual skills among limited sectors of the population. Yet old Russian culture, so rich in the aesthetic sphere, had tended to minimize or even oppose the use of abstract reason. Russia's Orthodox Church had never developed or shared in the scholastic tradition of the Latins, and the Mongol invasion had cut the country off from any effective participation in the Western European Renaissance.[2] Formal education and disciplined rational thought patterns first came to Russia as alien imports from the

West. Containing elements that were genuinely subversive of the existing culture, they were initially resisted by all classes of the population. Eventually the more important schools began to establish small but tenacious roots in Russian soil and to contribute to the flowering of a new and Western-influenced Russian culture—a culture, however, that was not always welcomed by its autocratic sponsors.

How did the autocracy approach the difficult task of introducing educational institutions into such an initially uncongenial environment? To what extent did its educational decisions make a real impact on Russia's evolving social and cultural patterns? What role did the schools play in shaping the attitudes and activities of their teachers and students, and to what extent did these new beliefs correspond either to the outlook of the autocracy or to the needs of a developing society?

In seeking to answer these questions, we shall present neither an even-handed survey of all aspects and time periods of tsarist education nor an exhaustive coverage of one particular area. Rather, what follows will be an extended interpretive essay focusing in turn on those two areas where educational policies and attitudes had the sharpest impact on Russia's social and cultural development. Part One will analyze autocratic approaches to education, and will argue that far from being completely predetermined, the huge social and cultural contrasts of late Imperial Russia were to a considerable extent the direct result of basic inconsistencies underlying tsarist educational policies. Part Two will focus on the outlook of Russian professors (or, as the majority of this group can more meaningfully be termed, the academic intelligentsia[3]), and will suggest that this outlook, as well as the universities which nurtured it, helped to foster an intellectual climate which, while highly beneficial to the flowering of Russian culture, was detrimental both to the political survival of the autocracy and to a more balanced development of Russian society.

There is a twofold advantage in analyzing separately and over a relatively long period of time the educational views of both autocratic officials and the academic intelligentsia. First, it enables one to see more clearly some of the weaknesses and internal inconsistencies that characterized the basic assumptions of each group as well as to understand and to appreciate the contexts within which these assumptions were formed. Second, and more importantly, it serves to highlight a fundamental agreement between the two groups which has been too often overlooked. They had very different goals, and their relations were often marked by hostility, but on the most basic premise of Russian educational policy—that a large proportion of the educational budget should be devoted to the establishment of Western-style academic institutions and the encouragement of pure research—they were in basic accord. It is the main theme of this work to question this common assumption, and to suggest that its implementation may well have hindered both the autocracy's goal of maintaining the autocratic tradition intact, and the academic intelligentsia's goal of promoting a liberalized, enlightened Russia.

# Part One

## THE AUTOCRACY AND THE DILEMMAS OF EDUCATION

THE HISTORY OF THE RUSSIAN EDUCATIONAL SYSTEM CAN BE CONVENIENTLY divided into two main periods. The time from Peter the Great to roughly 1900 was characterized by an autocratic monopoly over virtually all educational planning, initiatives, and administration. The rate of growth in enrollments and in the number of schools, although exhibiting striking differences among the primary, secondary, and higher educational sectors, was on the whole painfully slow during the eighteenth and nineteenth centuries. The relatively brief period from 1900 to the collapse of tsardom in 1917, on the other hand, was significantly different in both respects. Public pressure, which had vented itself sporadically since the 1860s, now became strong enough to create and consolidate a separate, if subordinate, public (as opposed to state-controlled) educational sector, and partially to influence educational policies adopted for the state schools. This development was accompanied by a sizeable increase in educational expenditures which led to a doubling of enrollments in all types of schools between 1900 and 1914.

As might be expected, historians have tended to give very different evaluations to the two periods. The eighteenth- and nineteenth-century tsars have received some praise for their recognition of the need to promote education and for the willingness to import Western-type schools to accomplish this goal, but those in the nineteenth century in particular have been generally castigated for their failure to move fast enough and for their seemingly inveterate tendency periodically to lapse from "progressive" into "reactionary" educational policies.[1]

Much more positive is the view of 1900–17. Most Western historians have hailed the educational policies of this period as a welcome if belated effort to correct previous inadequacies and as constituting a program which, had it been allowed to continue, would have in time resolved Russia's educational problems. The sociologist Nicholas S. Timasheff, who harbors extremely positive views of many aspects of late Imperial Russia, has argued that the drive to achieve universal public education, begun in 1908, was already by 1917 beginning to reduce the

2

tension which stemmed from the contrast between the educated few and the illiterate "people."[2] Even those who do not share Timasheff's optimism concerning the evolution of tsardom as a whole are inclined to grant that in the area of education at least, Russia was making great strides before the Revolution.[3] Indeed, the author of the most recent and most perceptive survey of tsarist education has concluded that, "whatever its failings in other areas — and they were massive — in general education tsardom was working hard, productively, and intelligently at the moment when military disaster retired it from history."[4]

The following analysis will draw somewhat different conclusions. We shall find, it is true, that autocratic educational policies before 1900 largely failed to meet the developing needs of the country — but for reasons that are rather different from those that have usually been put forth. And we shall find that despite the spectacular quantitative achievements of 1900-1917, Russia's basic educational problems were still not being realistically addressed during this period and that some, indeed, were being allowed to worsen.

# *1*

# AUTOCRATIC APPROACHES TO EDUCATION, 1700–1900

THERE WAS NO SINGLE APPROACH TO EDUCATION THAT WAS CONSISTENTLY followed by the tsars. Vacillation, indecision, and reversals were commonplace even within the confines of a single reign, let alone as the result of the succession from one ruler to the next. Highly placed ministers were sometimes given the tsar's blessing to adopt simultaneously within their own spheres of jurisdiction education policies based on contradictory principles. Yet it is nonetheless possible, with hindsight, to delineate four basic attitudes toward education which were held by the most important autocratic officials. They consisted of the conviction that the autocracy must not yield to society at large its monopoly over reform initiatives and administrative controls in the field of education (as well as other policy spheres); the deep-seated fear that social, political, and philosophical ideas originating in the West posed a clear and present danger to the political stability of the tsarist order; the recognition that if Russia were to compete in the international arena, her citizens needed skills that could only be furnished by an educational system; and, finally, a curious inferiority complex vis-à-vis the West which led to the adoption of educational and cultural institutions based on foreign models having remote utilitarian applications in Russia. These four attitudes do not cohabit easily with one another. Yet they could all be found, to a greater or lesser degree, in the intellectual makeup of most of the statesmen of Imperial Russia. How to devise an educational system which was consistent with these four attitudes was a problem that bedeviled some of the best official minds of the empire. An examination of each of these attitudes, as they manifested themselves between the years 1700 and 1900, will clarify the constraints within which educational planners labored as well as explain many of the peculiarities of the educational system that resulted.

## AUTOCRATIC INITIATIVE AND CONTROL

The greatest exponent of the principle of autocratic initiative was Peter the Great (1682–1725). Peter's efforts in education, like most of his reforms, were hampered by the indifference (if not downright hostility) of most of the population and by the lack of administrative machinery to enforce them. The Russian nobility was unresponsive to Peter's insistence that it become literate—a situation which Peter characteristically but ineffectively tried to meet by requiring all noble sons to pass a basic examination before they could marry, become officers, or be considered legal adults.[1]

Much more effective was his method of linking education to the service obligation which he had intensified for all nobility. The government would not only provide the schools free of cost, it would also compel the pupils to attend and pay them for doing so. "If the pupil was sent to school by the government, then study was for him service. For this service he received a salary; for failure to fulfill his duties he was subjected to penalties. In such a way, the responsibility of the pupil in no way differed from that of the grown man."[2]

For the next hundred years the autocracy and nobility sparred over the nature of the educational obligations that were to be imposed. Rather than continuing to oppose education outright, the leading families began to accept the need for some education, providing that it be organized on their own terms. They insisted that schools attended by their sons, unlike those founded by Peter, be exclusively noble in social composition and intellectually undemanding in curriculum. They won significant concessions in these respects from Peter's successors. As early as 1731 an exclusive aristocratic boarding school, known as the Cadet Corps, opened in St. Petersburg. It and others like it provided the nontechnical curriculum of an aristocratic finishing school, helping to endow a crude Russian nobility with a veneer of Western manners, and providing its graduates with significant advantages in state service assignments. Although poor provincial nobles pleaded for the widespread extension of the system into the countryside, it continued to cater primarily to the wealthier and better-placed noble families. By the nineteenth century the cadet corps system became exclusively military in orientation, while a new elite system of lyceums was created to train young nobles for the civil service. The most famous of these was the Imperial Lyceum at Tsarskoe Selo, which offered a six-year course that was in between the academic levels of a secondary school and a university. Together with the similarly structured School of Jurisprudence, founded in 1838, the Lyceum continued until 1917 to turn out small groups of aristocratic graduates who consistently reached the highest ranks of the bureaucracy.[3]

But although willing to make some important educational concessions to gentry sentiment, the tsars were determined, in addition, to establish a university network having the highest academic standards. The first functioning Russian university was founded in 1755 in Moscow. In order to encourage gentry attendance, an exclusively noble gymnasium and boardinghouse (*pansion*) were established in connection with the university. But in view of the gentry's well-known disinclination for serious educational endeavor, the autocrats did not hesitate to look elsewhere for talent. Moscow University itself, despite its noble *pansion,* was open to all estates except serfs, as were the schools projected by Catherine II (1762–96) and founded by Alexander I (1801–25).[4]

Perhaps the best example of the refusal of the autocracy to bow completely to local gentry pressure on educational questions is the founding of Kharkov University in the early years of the nineteenth century. The Kharkov nobility favored the establishment of a cadet corps school that would be open to gentry only, whereas Alexander I was bent on establishing a university on the same model as that in Moscow and as the one that was simultaneously being established in Kazan. V. N. Karazin, a Kharkov nobleman with high connections in St. Petersburg, undertook to negotiate what he hoped would be a compromise, in which the institution would be a university but with local gentry representation and a separate course in military science. His efforts were completely rebuffed by Alexander, and the resultant university was based on centralized principles making absolutely no concessions to local sentiment.[5]

Curiously enough, the autocratic insistence on maintaining the state's initiative did not result in an educational system that was either administratively or conceptually unified. Jurisdiction over various types of educational institutions was distributed among a number of different bureaucratic agencies, often having divergent outlooks and interests. General agreement that education should be government controlled and serve the interests of the state did not preclude vigorous debates at the highest bureaucratic levels over what those interests were and how they could best be achieved. Indeed, tsarist Russia was confronted with most of the same educational issues that faced those countries in which public and local decision-making was more widely developed. The main difference was not so much the nature of the issues that were debated, but rather the arena in which they were resolved. In Russia this arena was always the upper echelons of the central bureaucracy.

During the eighteenth century the single most important educational agency was the Holy Synod, the governing body of the Orthodox Church. The Synod, which functioned as an organ of the central government, administered a network of institutions, including parish schools, secondary-level seminaries, and a small number of theological academies. This network continued to exist until the Revolution. Its seminaries in particular played an important role in Russian education, producing many notable graduates (such as the bureaucratic reformer Michael Speranskii, the radical intellectual Nicholas Chernyshevskii, and the future Joseph Stalin) who did not pursue clerical careers. In the nineteenth century, however, the Church was overshadowed in educational administration by the newly created Ministry of Public Education, which was established, together with other ministries, as the result of sweeping reforms of central governmental administration in 1802 and 1810-11. The ministry received jurisdiction over the universities and most general secondary educational institutions, while sharing control over primary education with the Holy Synod. Nor were these the only governmental organs to become involved in education. The army maintained a network that included schools at all levels, from primary to higher educational institutions. A number of other ministries, including those of finance and transportation, established vocationally oriented secondary schools and technical institutes to train personnel needed by the military and the economy. During the reign of Nicholas I (1825-55) the Empress Dowager Marie established Section IV of His Majesty's Special Chancery to administer an elite secondary school system for girls. This network maintained its separate existence down to 1917 despite the development after 1858 of a parallel system of girls' gymnasia under the auspices of the Ministry of Public Education.

Jurisdictional jealousies sometimes intensified high-level education debates which would have been serious enough in any event. The most important was the momentous conflict under Alexander II (1855-81) between Dmitri Tolstoi as Minister of Education and Dmitri Miliutin as Minister of War. The debate came to a head in 1871-72, when Tolstoi introduced draft legislation, designed to implement his proclassicist policies in the Ministry of Education's school system, in the State Council for discussion and vote. With Miliutin leading the opposition, a majority of the council voted to reject Tolstoi's legislation—but Alexander exercised the sovereign's prerogative to disregard the State Council's opinion, and ordered that Tolstoi's projects be enacted into law.[6]

Despite this defeat, however, Miliutin was still able to determine the nature of those schools which were under the jurisdiction of his own War Ministry. The results were somewhat anomalous. The military secondary schools came to embody a more liberal spirit than those of the Education Ministry, and the army's Medical-Surgical Academy became the first Russian higher educational institution to admit women to a degree-granting program.[7]

But if the autocratic monopoly of educational initiative did not lead to either consistency or uniformity in educational policy, it did impart a certain bias to the structure of the educational network. The Russian educational system was built from the top down. Either lacking (in the eighteenth century) or distrusting (in the nineteenth) large numbers of individuals who could organize and staff primary and secondary schools at the local level, the autocracy concentrated its efforts on higher level institutions, which were easier and cheaper to establish and control and which seemed to promise more immediate returns in the production of qualified personnel. Although Russian conditions partially dictated such an approach, the extent of this structural bias as well as the type of institutions supported were more the result of choice than circumstance. Russia had an Academy of Sciences before she had a functioning university. By the early nineteenth century a university network had been established, but it was not until the middle of the century that the state began to spend as much on secondary schools as on universities. It was not until the beginning of the twentieth century that primary schools began to receive funds equal to those of the other sectors.[8]

Furthermore, within the secondary and higher sectors, both enrollment and budgetary priority went to the elite academic institutions rather than to the more practical schools. In 1887 there were more pupils enrolled in the classical gymnasia (70,921) than in the real-schulen (21,040) and municipal or district schools (44,163) combined.[9] At this time the Ministry of Education was spending 9 million rubles annually on its gymnasia and universities, while allotting a mere 2.2 million to its vocational schools and technical institutes.[10] Herein lies much of the explanation for the striking contrast in prerevolutionary Russia between a glittering scientific and cultural intelligentsia on the one hand and massive illiteracy and technical backwardness on the other.

## THE DANGERS OF EDUCATION

The tsars' determination to retain control over education throughout the nineteenth century stemmed not only from an anachronistic adherence to autocratic tradition, but also from a recognition of the potential danger that an educational system could harbor. If Peter the Great could be blissfully unaware of the threat to political stability which accompanied the widespread importation of Western ideas and institutions, his successors could not afford to be so complacent. Three events of the late eighteenth and early nineteenth centuries — the French Revolution, the Napoleonic invasion, and the Decembrist Revolt — had a searing mental impact on Russian autocrats and conservative thinkers, who were quick to single out materialistic, rationalistic, and democratic ideas from the West as the prime cause of these traumatic calamities. Catherine is said to have petulently smashed her personal bust of Voltaire upon learning of the execution of Louis XVI, and Alexander reportedly turned for the first time to Bible reading when Napoleon marched into Russia. The response of Nicholas I to the Decembrist uprising was more practical and more consequential in the long run. He sought to reinforce the political and social status quo by establishing a secret police network and intensifying a system of censorship designed to minimize the importation and spread of Western ideas. His Minister of Education, Sergei S. Uvarov, continued the expansion of the educational system, but endeavored to counteract its dangerous potentialities by impregnating it with an official ideology glorifying Orthodoxy, autocracy, and Russian nationality.

At the same time that the tsars were becoming convinced that the main threat to political stability came from Western ideas, their internal opponents were arriving at a very similar conclusion. With all its censorship and control, the reign of Nicholas I (1825–55) nonetheless witnessed the birth of the classical Russian intelligentsia. This group, totally alienated from existing Russian institutions, imbibed Western political and philosophical doctrines which slipped through the censorship, and indeed tended to regard these doctrines as in some sense a key to the subsequent transformation of Russia.

It is undeniable that the ideological foundations of tsarist autocracy were particularly vulnerable to rational analysis. Absolute autocratic power, rule by divine right, the influence of a servile and intellectually stagnant Orthodox Church, the deliberate perpetuation of a rigidly differentiated estate system even after the emancipation of the serfs in 1861 — all these official dogmas seemed to offend the rational, critical, and moral faculties which Western thought-systems were helping to develop in young Russian minds. But did it follow, as so many members of the intelligentsia were quick to assume, that Western ideas could serve not only as agents for the criticism of Russian reality, but also as the basis for effective new institutions of a reformist or revolutionary nature?

Equally questionable was the autocratic conviction that the educational system itself, quite apart from its surrounding political, social, and intellectual context, had a potentially decisive influence in molding the character and behavior of its charges. This principle was frequently carried to the extent of holding the policies of the Minister of Education responsible for the many outbreaks of revolutionary activity by educated youth in the nineteenth century. Thus, Dmitri Tolstoi became minister in 1866 after the attempted assassination of the tsar by a student drop-out discredited the educational policies of his predecessor. But he himself was asked to resign by Count Loris-Melikov in 1880 after the dynamiting of the Winter Palace, only to return to the government as Minister of the Interior after the assassination of Alexander II led to a new change of policies. Indeed, the position of Minister of Education was one of the most insecure posts in the Russian bureaucracy. During the period 1802-1917 no fewer than twenty-seven individuals occupied that position. Only the equally sensitive Ministry of the Interior had a higher turnover rate of ministers.[11]

It now seems clear that neither the importation of Western ideas nor the specific educational policies of the ministry *in themselves* caused the widespread disaffection that was so apparent among Russia's educated youth. It is more likely that a combination of the oppressive autocratic system and the implantation of Westernized elitist educational institutions produced an intellectual and institutional climate in which radical ideas of Western origin could take root and flourish.[12] The dangers to the autocracy from such an educational system, though often misunderstood, were nonetheless very real.

Under such circumstances it is hardly surprising that state officials occasionally indulged in anti-intellectual outbursts of repression against higher educational institutions. In the latter part of Alexander I's reign, education curator M. L. Magnitskii conducted an ideological purge of Kazan University on the professed grounds that "Godless university professors are distilling the atrocious poison of disbelief and of hate toward legitimate power for our unhappy youth."[13] As a response to the European revolutions of 1848, Nicholas I removed his Minister of Education, Uvarov, reduced university enrollments by one-quarter, and outlawed the teaching of European constitutional law and philosophy. In 1911 Education Minister L. A. Kasso, though himself a former professor of classics, arbitrarily precipitated the resignation of well over one hundred leading scientists and scholars from Moscow University.

But spasmodic repression was not the primary method utilized by the autocracy in its effort to counteract the dangers stemming from the educational system. More thoughtful men, such as Sergei Uvarov and Dmitri Tolstoi, became convinced that a strong educational system with high academic standards would pose little danger to the state if only centralized control were maintained over how the schools were administered, what the students were taught, and which social classes were enabled to attend. As a result, the "Tolstoi system," implemented in the early 1870s, featured an all-pervasive control and inspection of both schools and pupils, the imposition of a pedantic classicism as the curricular staple of the gymnasium, and the perpetuation of a highly elitist and differentiated primary-secondary network.

Tolstoi's most prized institutions were the gymnasia, and it was these that he subjected the most thoroughly to centralized control and supervision. Virtually all aspects of curricular and administrative affairs were decided at the ministerial level and dictated to all schools. In an effort to establish control over the moral conduct and political ideas of the students, Tolstoi called for the appointment of a special counselor (*nastavnik*), usually drawn from the ranks of the classics teachers, for each of the eight classes of the gymnasium. The duties of the counselor included becoming intimately acquainted with the character of each of his charges, and a favorable report from the counselor was an essential prerequisite for graduation. Nor was this supervision limited to the walls of the school itself. In 1874 Tolstoi issued rules for deportment of gymnasium pupils that were meant to apply to those who lived at home with their parents. They required pupils to participate periodically in the rituals of the Orthodox Church, return directly home after school, and not visit parks, libraries, theaters, or lecture halls without special permission.[14] During the 1870s Tolstoi also worked on drafting a new university statute, subsequently implemented in 1884, that contained a similar emphasis on centralized administrative control and student supervision.

A strong pillar of the Tolstoi system was the intensified emphasis placed on Latin and Greek in the centrally prescribed gymnasium curriculum. Pupils were to begin the study of Latin in the first course and Greek in the third, and indeed during the eight-year course more classroom hours were devoted to the study of these languages than to Russian. Although mathematics was highly emphasized, both the physical and the social sciences received very little attention.[15] Furthermore, Tolstoi insisted that in the teaching of Latin and Greek stress be placed on grammar and translation rather than on the study of classical literature (which, after all, frequently contained dangerous republican or even materialist views). Classes were to be conducted under a formal recitation method in which discussion of extraneous issues was prohibited. Academic standards were very high; a major part of the final examinations required the translation of difficult passages from Russian into Latin and Greek.[16]

Russian political and ideological conditions were primarily responsible for convincing Tolstoi of the virtues of classicism. One of the most disturbing phenomena of the 1860s, from the autocratic viewpoint, had been the movement of intellectual nihilism that had spread so widely among Russia's urban youth. Most of the leading lights of this movement had an irregular educational background, and did not always thoroughly understand the tenets of natural science which formed the crux of their world view. Tolstoi thought that his curriculum would help to steer the elite youth of the country away from this type of orientation mainly in two ways. First, its compulsory nature and strenuous academic rigor would put an end to the hitherto predominant tendency of many youth to pick up their education here and there, in "bits and pieces."[17] Second, its emphasis on classical languages and abstract mathematics would insulate immature minds from subjects such as the natural and social sciences, which Tolstoi believed led too easily to incorrect and improper social and political generalizations.

A final way in which Tolstoi sought to minimize the dangers which public education posed for the autocracy was by accentuating the already existing differentiation and elitist bias of the ministry's primary-secondary school network. This system, as modified by Tolstoi, consisted of four major components. At the top of the hierarchy stood the eight-year gymnasium, the main function of which was to prepare its pupils for university study. Indeed, the state-administered maturity exam served simultaneously as a final examination for the gymnasium and entrance exam for the university.[18] Next in order of prestige came the realschule, which prepared some of its pupils for entrance to non-university higher educational institutions while providing others with terminal training in various specialities. Dmitri Miliutin and other "official liberals" had attempted without success to establish the realschule as an academic equal to the gymnasium with the right to send its graduates to the university. Nonetheless, its first four years in particular maintained equally high academic standards, though without instruction in classical languages. Much more modest in terms of standards and costs were the six-year municipal schools and, *a fortiori,* the two- to four-year village primary schools.

None of the four major types of schools was designed to lead directly into another. The gymnasium was complete in itself, and since it began Latin instruction in the first course, those who transferred to it from outlying schools had either to undergo expensive tutoring or waste time by starting in the first class. Similarly, there was no easy transfer from the primary school to the municipal school. Consequently, those who lived some distance from the better types of schools and were unable to afford extra tutoring or urban lodging for their children found themselves at a distinct disadvantage.

Why did Tolstoi favor such a segmented and highly structured educational network? He was convinced that disaffected and hence dangerous students were most likely to come from the ranks of the ill-prepared and undermotivated. The gymnasium, with its strict controls and stiff classical curriculum, was the school most likely to weed out such pupils before they reached the university level. By requiring virtually all incoming university students to have coped successfully with several long, hard years of gymnasium study, Tolstoi thought he could control the type of students who reached the pinnacle of the educational system.

Another by-product of the differentiated school network was that it hindered, though by no means prevented, social mobility. Tolstoi was probably not displeased with this result, but unlike many of his more conservative colleagues, he did not favor formal admission restrictions based on religion, nationality, or social class, nor did he reduce the number of state stipends available to needy university students. He received the enthusiastic applause of Jewish leaders in Kherson when he proudly proclaimed, "We make only one distinction among pupils—a distinction on the basis of merit.... Our gymnasia must produce aristocrats, but what kind? Aristocrats of the mind, aristocrats of knowledge, aristocrats of labor. May God grant that we gain more such aristocrats."[19]

Tolstoi's words were not pure bluster. He had encouraged increased Jewish involvement in the state school system, and during his tenure the proportion of the gentry class in the elite educational institutions actually declined. It was under his successor, Ivan Delianov, Minister of Education from 1882 to 1898, that Jewish and lower middle-class pupils were officially perceived to constitute a menace to the Russian body politic.

The main impetus for the change in policy came not from Delianov himself, a career official in the ministry who seems to have had few enduring principles of his own, but from Constantine Pobedonostsev, who was at that time Ober-Procurator of the Holy Synod, and who had proposed to Tsar Alexander III (1881–94) that Delianov be appointed minister. Contemporaries agreed that Delianov was directly under the influence of Pobedonostsev and the strongly conservative publicist M. N. Katkov.[20] These men had a much dimmer view than Tolstoi of Western intellectual doctrines and of the role of education in general. Scornful of those "doctrinaires of science" who treat "abstract propositions" as "indisputable axioms," Pobedonostsev argued that too much education was liable to lead children "to the temptation of vanity and conceit," thereby endangering the social stability of the state.[21]

Pobedonostsev and Delianov did not, however, propose to dismantle or weaken the academic content of the existing gymnasia and universities. These institutions retained their rigorous and European-oriented intellectual standards until the end of the empire. Instead, they sought to restrict the number of students admitted, and implemented discriminatory measures in the admissions process that favored upper-class Orthodox Great Russians over national-religious minorities and middle- or lower-class aspirants. For those left out of the elite system, they favored schools which were less intellectual in approach and which they hoped would prepare pupils to assume their "proper" station in life.

Pobedonostsev's first major step was to reestablish a separate network of primary schools under the jurisdiction of the Holy Synod rather than the Ministry of Education. Although Tolstoi had come to the conclusion that the intellectual level of priests and other church personnel was too low to enable them to be suitable teachers, Pobedonostsev believed that the moral and religious benefits of a church education would outweigh any intellectual deficiencies. The church network, which always remained smaller than the ministry system, grew quite rapidly until 1900, after which it quickly lost ground to the ministry schools.[22]

A second major step was to increase the role of the Ministry of Education in vocational education — a move that was dictated more by administrative and political concerns than by a desire to assist the growing industrial economy. In 1881 all the vocational schools under the relatively liberal Ministry of Finance were transferred to the Ministry of Education, which proceeded to increase administrative controls over the schools. For example, the St. Petersburg Technological Institute, one of the most important schools transferred, received a new charter in 1887 which applied to it most of the restrictions contained in the university charter of 1884.[23]

In addition to acquiring jurisdiction over many existing schools, the Ministry of Education established a completely new and comprehensive system of vocational schools by a statute of 1888. The statute represented a modified version of a plan that had been elaborated by Ivan Vyshnegradskii, a strong proponent of vocational education who became Minister of Finance in 1887. The 1888 statute called for the establishment, alongside the higher technical institutes already in existence, of three types of schools: middle technical schools to produce technicians, lower technical schools to produce skilled foremen, and crafts and industry schools to produce skilled workmen. But whereas Vyshnegradskii had stressed the importance of a strong general educational component, this aspect was minimized in the Ministry of Education's implementation of the project. The motivation of Delianov and

Pobedonostsev in establishing the new vocational network stemmed at least as much from political as from economic or educational concerns. They hoped that the new system would lure the less privileged classes away from the more academically oriented gymnasia and realschulen. It was this political twist that soured much of public opinion toward the schools and resulted in their being less successful than they otherwise might have been.[24]

But far and away the most unpopular educational measures undertaken by Delianov and Pobedonostsev were the imposition of Jewish quotas and the issuance of the "cooks' circular," which directed local gymnasium authorities to discriminate in their admissions policies against the "children of coachmen, menials, cooks, washerwomen, small shopkeepers, and the like." The Jewish quotas, which applied to realschulen and universities as well as gymnasia, were set at 10 percent of the student body in the Pale of Settlement, 5 percent elsewhere, and 3 percent in the capital cities of Moscow and St. Petersburg. Although frequently evaded by local authorities, they remained in force until 1917 and greatly restricted the educational opportunities of many Jewish children. The impact of the cooks' circular is more difficult to measure, in part because there was a wide variation of results in different regions. In the short run the main goals — a reduction in the dropout rate, a contraction in enrollment, and an increase in the proportion of students from privileged classes — seem to have been achieved. Between 1881 and 1894 the enrollment of boys' gymnasia decreased from 65,800 to 62,900, while the percentage of pupils from the nobility and high bureaucracy increased from 47.5 percent to 56.4 percent. But in the long run, efforts to maintain noble predominance in the gymnasia were doomed to failure, if only because most schools were located in the cities, a fact which in itself favored the urban middle classes over that part of the gentry which resided in the countryside. After 1894 the trends induced by the cooks' circular reversed themselves, and by 1913 enrollments had climbed to 152,000, while gentry representation had declined to 32.5 percent.[25]

These, then, were the ways in which tsarist officials endeavored to cope with the dangers posed by an expanding educational system. Were they effective? To answer that question one need only observe that both in the late 1870s and the late 1890s, toward the end of the tenures of Tolstoi and Delianov respectively, student demonstrations, riots, and participation in revolutionary movements were at their height. Whether different educational policies might have succeeded in stemming the tide of student disaffection is a debatable issue; that the policies actually implemented clearly failed to do so is not. In fact, the conviction that a formal education system inevitably brought with it unwelcome ideas and subversive activities only seemed to receive stronger and stronger confirmation as the century progressed. Viewed in this perspective, one might ask, not why did the autocracy move so slowly to spread education in Russia, but indeed, why did it move so fast?

## THE USES OF EDUCATION

The reasons why authorities were willing to promote a high-quality educational system at the great risk of encouraging subversion are not difficult to find. To most it was clear that the West posed dangerous challenges to the well-being of Russia, challenges which could be met only by an educated response. Education might well bring potential dangers from within, but the lack of education most certainly would bring real dangers from without. Exactly how various authorities perceived these external dangers and what kinds of response they recommended are questions worthy of brief examination.

Probably the first official to act on such sentiments was Metropolitan Peter Mogila, who founded the Kievan Academy in 1632, thirty-five years before Kiev came under Muscovite control. Kiev at that time was located on the western fringe of Orthodox civilization, in direct contact and conflict with Catholic, Uniat, and Protestant elements of eastern Europe. Mogila's goal was to help defend Orthodoxy by training graduates who would be intellectually equipped to combat both Jesuits and Protestants on their own ground of theological debate. Many graduates of his academy migrated to Moscow, where they became major figures in the internal Orthodox struggles that shook Muscovy at this time and where they helped to establish, by the end of the century, a theological academy in Moscow itself.[26]

Although Peter the Great sponsored the further expansion of a church educational network based on the principles of the Kievan Academy, his primary goals were quite different from those of Mogila. He was determined above all else to speed the adoption of Western technique in the Russian military and government. His School of Mathematical and Navigational Sciences, founded in 1701, was soon followed by engineering and artillery institutes and a system of "cipher schools" designed to spread knowledge of arithmetic and geometry throughout the Russian Empire.[27]

Nonetheless, a certain continuity in motivation between the efforts of Mogila and Peter has been rightly stressed by the historian Miliukov.

> In such a manner, in addition to a professional school for theology, there arose in Moscow a professional school for naval

science. The government's view concerning the goal of education had still not changed. Both now, as formerly, learning
[*nauka*] and the school were to serve the practical needs of the
state. Only the understanding of those needs had changed:
instead of the correction of church books and the preservation
of the faith, the concern now was on the reform of the army
and the fleet.[28]

The Russian civil service, no less than the military, also needed
trained, competent personnel. Peter attempted to meet this need by
arranging the higher-level bureaucratic positions on a fourteen-rung
hierarchy called the table of ranks, with promotions to be based on
merit and seniority. By the early nineteenth century, government reformers came up with the idea of linking position on the table of ranks
to formal educational credentials. The first effort in this direction
failed. An 1809 law inspired by Speranskii sought to require all officials
to pass examinations before being promoted to both the eighth and fifth
ranks, but it faced such intense gentry opposition that it became a dead
letter after Speranskii's fall from grace in 1812. A similar objective,
however, was successfully achieved by a measure which granted to
graduates of universities, gymnasia, and special schools such as the
Imperial Lyceum the right to enter the table of ranks at a level higher
than that open to nongraduates. By offering a tangible reward for
educational achievement, this measure not only stimulated enrollments,
but also helped to raise the standards of the bureaucracy. Education
became a key to advancement in government service. By mid-century
most of the high-level bureaucrats continued to be hereditary nobles,
but formal educational experience was a more common characteristic
of this group than either wealth or inherited social status. Even appointment to the lowly chancery clerkship (consisting of those positions below
the fourteenth rung of the table of ranks) was based after 1828 on
secondary or at least primary school credentials.[29]

The Russian debacle in the Crimean War (1854–56) served to re-
awaken the conviction that Russia's stature as a military power was
directly related to her educational system. "If our enemies triumph over
us, it is due solely to the superiority of their knowledge," stated Minister
of Education A. S. Norov, an appointee of the conservative Nicholas I.[30]
Nor was his an isolated view. Among the very first policies undertaken
by Alexander II after his accession in 1855 were measures to enlarge and
improve the universities. An innovative article on educational reform by
N. I. Pirogov was published immediately following the war by the
official journal of the Department of the Navy.[31] The link between

education and military might was further cemented in many Russian minds by the victory of educated Prussia over Austria in 1866.

The use of education to propagandize Russian cultural and national values in areas of ethnically and religiously mixed populations was also not overlooked in the nineteenth century. As in Mogila's time, the main locale was the western borderlands, but the major instrumentalities were now universities and gymnasia rather than theological academies. After the Polish revolt of 1830, universities at Warsaw and Vilnius were closed and in effect replaced by a newly founded and strongly Russianized university at Kiev. Uvarov minced no words when he referred to the new institution as "an intellectual fortress" with the goal of "suppressing the spirit of a separate Polish nationality and merging it with the general Russian spirit."[32] A new higher educational institution that opened in Warsaw in the early 1860s became completely Russianized after the 1863 revolt. Many new gymnasia and other types of schools, in which Russian was the official language of instruction, were deliberately planted in Poland in particular and in the western lands in general.

Nor were the South Slavs forgotten. In the aftermath of the Crimean War, the liberal educator Pirogov urged the founding of a university in Odessa for the prime purpose of expanding Russia's cultural influence among the Orthodox Slavs of the Balkans. At that time, wrote Pirogov, Balkan youth had no choice but to attend universities in the West, where they came under the influence of either Catholicism or freethinking. A nearby Russian university would, he thought, be a great help in stemming this growing Western influence.[33] In this respect at least, the tsarist government saw fit to follow Pirogov's advice, and in 1865 the Richelieu Lyceum in Odessa was transformed into the New-Russian (*Novorossiiskii*) University.

The eastern areas of the empire, where national and cultural conflicts were much less intense, received correspondingly less favorable treatment. Siberia, with 70 percent of the territory and 11 percent of the population, had to wait until 1887 for its first university, and central Asia until 1920. Still more indicative of official policy is the fact that, aside from the capital cities of Petersburg and Moscow, even the Great Russian provinces of central European Russia were slighted in favor of the western borderlands in terms of gymnasium and realschule facilities —a situation which caused considerable concern to liberal nationalists among the Russian public when it came to light in the years after 1905.[34]

A final way in which the autocracy sought to utilize education was to promote economic growth. As early as 1773 the Corps of Mining Cadets (subsequently the Mining Institute) was established, and in 1809 the Chief Administration of Transportation founded an Institute of Transportation Engineers, modeled on the Parisian *École Polytechnique*. Finance Minister Egor Kankrin virtually single-handedly established a secondary technical school in 1828 that thirty-four years later was upgraded to become the St. Petersburg Technological Institute. Nonetheless, the cause of technical education languished during the thirties, forties, and fifties.[35] Only slight progress was made in subsequent decades, and by the end of the century the government was being urged to increase its spending on vocational education by ten times.[36] In certain quarters an awareness was growing of the great need not only for more high-level technical specialists, but also for increased middle-level technical training and the introduction of at least some general education for all workers at industrial plants. The point was put most forcefully by I. A. Vyshnegradskii, who had been professor and director of the St. Petersburg Technological Institute in the 1870s and Minister of Finance in the 1880s:

> Our industry...is involved in a bitter struggle against foreign production in which our competitors can rely upon an element of workers with a relatively high general education and special training. Those workers considerably exceed, both in terms of the quality of the products and speed of production, the performance of the uneducated people who constitute the majority of the work force in our industrial plants, so that our industry has to conduct its struggle against foreign competition equipped with inferior weapons, and this of course leads to economic defeats. Because of all these circumstances, both the areas of general education and of special training of Russian workers call for the most energetic and urgent measures on the part of the government.[37]

The problems confronting Russian educational planners can now be viewed in clearer perspective. A formal educational system was needed to fulfill clearly delineated political, cultural, military, and economic functions that would strengthen the state against Western competition. This in itself would have proved a challenging task, for it was difficult to specify then, just as it is today, precisely what kind of schooling is most likely to produce the best soldiers, workers, professionals, or civil servants. The task was further complicated by the fact that, because of Russian tradition and political realities, the educational system had to be conceived, implemented, and controlled by a small group of officials at the center, and had to be carefully tailored to minimize as much as possible its inherently subversive potentialities.

Nonetheless, it is not inconceivable that a relatively well-functioning educational system, by and large responsive to the demands placed upon it, might have been constructed within the framework of these assumptions and constraints. What turned a highly difficult task into a virtually impossible one was the pervasiveness of yet a fourth consideration in the minds of many tsarist statesmen: the conviction that Russian education should be based on the seemingly most advanced European models.

## THE ALLURE OF THE WEST

That Russians should have turned to the West for educational ideas and models is hardly surprising. Modern formal education was, after all, a Western development, with no precedents in old Russian culture. But the West was not a unitary phenomenon; there were many different models that might have been imitated or adapted. What is noteworthy, then, is the propensity to select for emulation precisely those institutions that would seem to have the least applicability to Russian needs. It was as though when planning the nature of what were to become the country's most important educational institutions, officials forgot the real uses to which the institutions were to be put and let themselves be guided instead by ephemeral considerations of increasing Russian prestige in the eyes of Europe.

Although Peter the Great is often regarded as an extremely pragmatic tsar, the prestige motive is clearly evident in his founding of the Russian Academy of Sciences, which was to become one of the most nonutilitarian institutions in Russian history. To be sure, Peter's attitude toward science was greatly influenced by Leibniz, who in founding the Berlin Academy in 1700 had stressed the direct service science could render to the state. Yet both the circumstances of its founding and the subsequent development of the academy in Russia suggest that Peter's hunger for European prestige impelled him to establish an institution that was basically unsuited to Russia's needs. Peter cherished his reputation among European savants as a mighty foe of ignorance and champion of rationality, a reputation that was crowned by his election to a full membership in the Paris Academy of Sciences in 1717. In drawing up plans for his own academy, Peter rejected the advice of the German natural scientist Christian Wolff that, in view of Russian conditions, it would be more feasible to concentrate on spreading knowledge throughout the empire rather than attempting to further it by elaborate research efforts. Wolff suggested that the tsar establish a univeristy rather than an academy, and recruit able teachers rather than eminent researchers. Peter acquiesced only to the extent of including plans for a university and gymnasium in his projected academy; he insisted that the academician-professors be recruited from the most prominent scholars and scientists of Europe. He was convinced that the establishment of a scientific research institution in Russia "would earn us respect and honor in Europe" and refute the widespread belief that "we are barbarians who disregard science."[38]

Russia's Academy of Science did in fact become the center for internationally important research and scholarship in the eighteenth and nineteenth centuries, and gave an undeniable boost to the development of science in Russia. But its orientation from the outset was more theoretical than practical, and it never (until World War I) functioned as a center of expertise available to the government. One of its most distinguished eighteenth-century members, the world famous mathematician Leonhard Euler, preferred to publish his treatises of an applied character under the auspices of the Berlin Academy, where there was more demand for them, while choosing St. Petersburg to publish his more theoretical works.[39]

Russian proficiency in pure science was intensified in the nineteenth century. The two most important ministers of education, Uvarov and Tolstoi, were themselves scholars in their own right, and each of them increased governmental funding of the Academy of Sciences, astronomical observatories, and central research libraries. Despite Tolstoi's opposition to the teaching of natural science in the gymnasia, he strongly supported scientific laboratories and research facilities at the university level, and encouraged the formation of scientific associations and the periodic convening of congresses. Much of his motivation stemmed from his belief that a more academically rigorous educational system would provide its students with less time and inclination for radical pursuits (a belief, incidentally, which was doomed to disappointment). But he was also deeply motivated by the conviction that Russia must end her humiliating backward position with regard to western Europe. "We shall not be forever the blind follower of the foreigner," he stated at an 1869 congress of Russian scientists, "but... we shall also be in a position to furnish Europe with the fruits of Russian thought, of Russian genius. In the world of learning, just as in the world of politics, Russia's international relations will be based only on complete equality."[40]

Western learning, however, embraced a number of different fields, including technology as well as mathematics or classical Greek. Yet the academy was relatively indifferent to technical subjects, and just as Russia was making impressive strides in pure science, she was falling further and further behind the West in areas of applied science. Thus, as one historian has pointed out, Russia chose to compete in that area of science which, at her level of development, promised the least benefit to her economy.[41]

Nor can it be said that the academy served as a fountainhead for the development of Russian culture and education. It was unable even to keep alive its own university and gymnasium, both of which ceased to exist soon after their founding due to lack of students. It continued to be dominated by foreigners until well into the nineteenth century — a domination that was frequently resented even by the Europeanized Russian academic intelligentsia. It did relatively little, compared to the universities, to disseminate ideas among the educated public as a whole.[42]

If the universities were slightly more integrated with Russian society than the academy, they nonetheless had a very similar origin and orientation. Although Moscow University had been founded in 1755, the Russian university system as a whole was established, on the basis of both French and German models, during the reign of Alexander I. Faced with the same staffing problem that Peter had encountered almost a century before, Alexander had to recruit most of the professors for the new universities from abroad. The European orientation of his project soon drew sharp criticism from Nicholas Karamzin, a conservative historian and literary figure who had initially praised Alexander's efforts to expand education in Russia. Karamzin wrote:

> The professors have been invited before there were students to hear them, and though many of these scholars are prominent, few are really useful; for the students, being but poorly acquainted with Latin, are unable to understand these foreign instructors, and are so few in number that the latter lose all desire to appear in class. The trouble is that we have built our universities on the German model, forgetting that conditions in Russia are different.... The constructing and purchasing of buildings for universities, the founding of libraries, cabinets, and scholarly societies, and the calling of famous astronomers and philologists from abroad — all this is throwing dust in the eyes. What subjects are not being taught today even at such places as Kharkov and Kazan! And this at a time when it takes the utmost effort to find in Moscow a teacher of Russian, when it is virtually impossible to find in the whole country a hundred men who know thoroughly the rules of orthography, when we lack a decent grammar, when imperial decrees make improper use of words....[43]

Karamzin went on to attack Speranskii's law of 1809, which required civil servants to present a certificate of university studies or pass an examination before they could be promoted beyond a certain rank.

> In the past, functionaries of the most enlightened states had been required to know only what was essential to their work: the engineer, engineering, the judge, law, and so on. But in Russia, the official presiding in the Civil Court must know Homer and Theocritus, the Senate Secretary—the properties of oxygen and all the gases, the Deputy Governor—Pythagorean geometry, the superintendent of a lunatic asylum—Roman law, or else they will end their days as Collegiate or Titular Counselors. Neither forty years of state service, nor important accomplishments exempt one from the obligation of having to learn things which are entirely alien and useless for Russians.[44]

It is easy to dismiss Karamzin as being motivated by a dislike for Speranskii and a desire to defend gentry interests. Furthermore, the gentry's well-known attachment to the undemanding cadet corps schools, to say nothing of the downright anti-intellectualism of a Magnitskii, do not offer much evidence of the existence of a realistic educational alternative more rooted in Russian needs. It was precisely the autocracy's determination to link service prerogatives with educational credentials that persuaded a hitherto reluctant gentry class to educate itself.

Nonetheless, there was considerable truth in Karamzin's critique. Efforts to import wholesale a foreign university system often led to farcical results in early nineteenth-century Russia.[45] More importantly, he raised a question which too few were willing to face: Granted that education was necessary to improve the competence of Russian officials, shouldn't we devise a system specifically tailored to meet Russian needs, rather than blindly imitating certain Western practices?

His advice was not taken. After considerable indecisiveness in the latter part of Alexander I's reign, Sergei Uvarov restored and Dmitri Tolstoi reinforced an educational system which, like the French, was highly centralized, and like the German, was capped by universities devoted to the advancement and dissemination of pure knowledge in accordance with European academic traditions. From one perspective, this decision can be regarded as felicitous. By the 1860s Russian universities had outgrown their earlier ungainliness, and were engaged in serious, high-level academic study. No longer did frustrated foreign professors have to cope with uncouth and uncomprehending provincial youth. Moscow University in particular had, as early as the 1830s and

1840s, begun to serve as a seed-bed for national culture, a breeding ground for the small but highly cultured and influential Russian intelligentsia. In the second half of the century, Russian scholars and scientists became participating members of the international academic community, and leadership of Russian "society" (*obshchestvo*) was assumed by well-educated persons familiar with European culture and accustomed to expressing themselves in terms of Western concepts and ideologies.

But if one takes the point of view of the interests of the autocracy, a very different evaluation must be made. In the first place, the application of German principles of university organization in the Russian context helped to produce a disaffected intelligentsia, and therefore tended to augment rather than diminish the dangers which the educational system posed for the regime. Secondly, the universities' stress on pure learning did not provide the country's elite youth with the skills which the empire so desperately needed. Was the curriculum of the juridical faculties, with its emphasis on Roman law, really the most appropriate training for a future Russian civil servant?

In some ways the Russian university system had a less practical orientation than its German counterpart. In Germany, entry into most professions as well as into civil service positions was strictly regulated by a system of state examinations. Although professors sat on the examining boards, frequently in collaboration with practicing specialists in the field, the state examination system was completely separate from the requirements for a university diploma. Indeed, a diploma was usually a prerequisite to taking a state examination, which had a more general and practical orientation than the university exams. The university diploma was regarded as demonstrating the student's ability to master a specialized field of pure knowledge, whereas the purpose of the state examination was to test his capacity to perform a particular job. Frequently, the state examination consisted of two parts. If the student passed the first part, he was placed in an apprenticeship position for a year and then required to pass a second test, based on his year's experience, before being granted permanent employment.[46]

In Russia the 1884 university charter contained a provision for state examinations that was superficially similar to but in reality quite different from the German system. The Russian state examinations were synonymous with the final examinations for a university diploma. The chairman of each examining committee was required to be from another university, but aside from an occasional official from the Ministry of Education, all the other examiners were the student's own professors. Upon passing the examination, the student automatically received the right to enter the civil service at a highly preferential rank. The system gave the ministry considerable control over both curricula and the examination questions. But this control was used to enforce political and ideological conformity in the lecture hall rather than to impart a professional or vocational orientation to the curriculum, and the system of state examinations was roundly criticized by most professors as resulting only in intellectual stultification and increased red tape.[47]

Tolstoi's classical gymnasia present a final case study of the ways in which an enthusiasm for certain Western models resulted in the adoption of educational institutions completely unsuited to Russia's needs. European educators had traditionally regarded the classics as the only proper basis for a truly liberal education, a view which though under continual attack from mid-century, continued to prevail in most countries for many more decades. Quite well informed about European educational developments, Tolstoi was particularly impressed by the Prussian system, in which the classical gymnasium remained until 1901 virtually the only avenue to university study. Although he introduced some important changes, it was thus the Prussian gymnasium and realschule that served as the basic models for the Russian institutions he established.[48]

The emphasis on Latin, Greek, and mathematics served not only to squeeze the natural sciences out of the gymnasium curriculum, but also greatly to restrict the amount of time its pupils, who were being groomed to take over the leading administrative and professional positions in the empire, could devote to the study of the Russian language, history, and institutions. Tolstoi welcomed this bias, in part because it presented less opportunity in the classroom for the discussion of controversial political or ideological topics. Yet the result was not without considerable irony. The autocracy was deliberately expanding an educational system which it needed on utilitarian grounds while at the same time making sure that the curricula of the most prestigious schools would be as nonutilitarian as possible. The potential dangers of education were being given priority over its potential uses. Yet why then have an educational system at all?

Tolstoi was no fool, and we must assume that he sincerely believed in the inherent pedagogical value of classicism as well as in its abilities to combat radicalism. It seemed to be producing men of strong character and leadership abilities in England and Germany; why should it not do the same in Russia? Tolstoi, the most influential education minister in the nineteenth century, was one of the least concerned with pragmatic, vocational goals. Criticizing the tendency of parents to value an education only for the careers it would lead to, he said, "The system of classical education does not in itself produce either a civil servant or an officer; it produces a human being [*chelovek*], and therefore the system is called humanistic. A well brought-up person will be useful in any field of endeavor."[49]

One might well ask whether the highly authoritarian, pedantic, and routinized atmosphere of the Tolstoi gymnasium didn't snuff out the humanizing aspect of classical studies. Or, to go further, whether the study of other academic subjects might yield equally humanistic results while laying a foundation of knowledge that would be much more applicable to Russian conditions. Or, finally, whether the very effort to transplant educational institutions from one society to another was misguided because the actual functioning of such institutions is invariably determined as much by their many invisible ties with the society in which they have developed as by their more formal, transferable characteristics.

One person who did ask these questions — and was removed from several teaching positions for his pains — was the mid-century educator K. D. Ushinskii. Himself a graduate of Western-oriented Moscow University and a pioneer in the scholarly field of comparative education, Ushinskii argued that the educational ideas of each people are permeated with their own national spirit, and that any effort to transfer them from one country to another would bring only their dead form, not their living content. "In order to lead public education on a direct and proper path," he wrote, "one must examine not what is necessary for Germany, France, England, etc., or what has been done or is being done there, but what is necessary for Russia in her present condition, what is compatible with her historical traditions, with the spirit and needs of her...whole people, from the small to the great." Ushinskii believed that primary schools should be organized not by central or provincial authorities, but by the local people themselves. A strong foe of classical education, he insisted that the native language should form the core of the curriculum, followed in importance by the natural sciences, history, geography, and mathematics. He believed that children learned best when they studied things with which they were in direct contact, rather than subjects completely removed from their everyday existence. Not only the children themselves, but Russia would benefit from such a pedagogical approach. In a strong rebuttal to Tolstoi, he argued, "At the present time we need most of all not Hellenists or Latinists, but zemstvo and governmental leaders, factory owners, engineers, manufacturers, farmers, and other *real people*."[50]

Ushinskii's sensible approach was rejected by the officialdom and the

Westernized intelligentsia alike. In summary, some of the repercussions of the contrary official policy should be noted. The imported universities (of which Ushinskii approved, it must be noted) helped to produce a cultivated but unskilled and generally disaffected intelligentsia. The Europeanized content of the education inevitably tended to widen the existing separation in outlook and attitude between the educated few and the uneducated masses. The concentration of scarce educational resources on elite secondary and higher schools, rather than on a more balanced apportionment among the primary, secondary, and higher sectors, served to intensify rather than reduce that immense cultural disparity between city and countryside which had begun in the eighteenth century and was to provoke such turmoil in the twentieth.

Why did normally hard-headed — and by no means unintelligent — officials adopt such a policy? The pattern has since been repeated many times by developing nations. Important statesmen, even while they vehemently denounced political and philosophical principles which they associated with the West, found themselves beguiled by aspects of a seemingly superior civilization. Although Pobedonostsev and some of the officials under Nicholas II form an exception to this rule, even they did not alter or eliminate the elite Westernized schools, but tried only to restrict and regulate those who would attend them. It was thus the allure of the West that prompted tsarist officials unwittingly to adopt policies which actually increased the dangers while reducing the uses of the educational system they were intent on promoting.

# 2

# ERRATIC DYNAMISM, 1900-17

THE DEATH IN OFFICE OF IVAN DELIANOV IN 1898 MARKS A TURNING POINT
in the development of Russian education. The policies of Tolstoi and of
Pobedonostsev and Delianov had engendered bitter opposition among
teachers, pupils, and much of the educated public as a whole. But these
ministers could well afford to ignore such opposition, which at first was
weak in numbers, disunited, and unrecognized. While they were in
office, real threats to the continuation of their programs came not from
social forces at large, but from "official liberals" in high governmental
positions and from the possible displeasure of the sovereign. By the end
of the century, however, this situation had changed considerably. Partly
due to the recent educational expansion (which had been furthered by
Tolstoi's own policies), and partly due to the rapid economic development of the 1880s and 1890s, a growing professional middle class
emerged which began to press for changes in the autocratic political
system in general and in the Tolstoi and Pobedonostsev educational
policies in particular.

Faced with this challenge, the autocracy entered into a new period
which was marked by three main characteristics. First, there was a
dramatic expansion of enrollments in all types of schools. Secondly,
reluctant approval was given to certain public initiatives in the educational sphere, and as a result one can detect for the first time a distinctly
public, as opposed to autocratic, impact on the size and shape of the
overall educational network. Thirdly, autocratic insecurity, exacer-
bated by the revolution of 1905, reached new heights, as periods of
public concession were followed by acts of strict repression.

Did these new developments help to resolve the inconsistencies that
had characterized autocratic policies, and to rectify the existing im-
balances of the educational network? Did the liberal public, as a whole,
have a better grasp of Russia's educational problems than the tsars and
their ministers? Was the quantitative growth in education accompanied
by equally significant changes in the types of schools and curricula that
were made available? Did the challenge of the liberal public force the

29

autocracy to undertake a fundamental reconsideration of its educational goals and priorities? These are the questions we must ask as we turn to a closer examination of the period in question.

## THE LIBERAL IMPACT ON RUSSIAN EDUCATION

Let us first examine the educational program and demands of the liberal public opinion at this time, in particular as they relate to the four autocratic approaches to education that have already been described. The principle of autocratic initiative and control was the *bête noire* of Russian liberals. Although the extent to which centralized political power should be shared was an issue on which thoughtful Russians could and did differ, the demand for far greater autonomy from autocratic control in the nonpolitical areas of social, economic, and cultural life was one that commanded widespread and vehement support from the liberal public. This demand was made by people at all levels of education: professors wanted a greater role in deciding university affairs; secondary school directors and teachers pleaded for greater autonomy within their classrooms; zemstvos and municipal dumas sought more control over the primary schools within their jurisdiction. Particularly unenviable was the position of the gymnasium teacher, who not only was forced to teach without the slightest deviation from centrally prescribed curriculum materials, but also was required to employ at all times a formal and arid recitation method in the classroom. A 1905 manifesto of the newly formed Union of Secondary School Teachers of St. Petersburg decried the existing constraints on their activities as teachers.

> Completely lacking confidence in the pedagogical tact of the teacher, the system vetoes informal relations with the pupils, thereby annulling the opportunity for a varied and sophisticated discussion of academic questions and current issues. This political tendency has been especially harmful to the teaching of history and literature, eliminating the vital and serious issues, representing the rest in a false and superficial light. Censorship of the teacher's speech is closely bound to censorship of textbooks, which, while depriving the instructor of the right to select material for reading and study, floods the schools with mediocre, tendentious textbooks. Restricted in his teaching, the teacher is subjected to strict supervision of his life outside the school. Any contribution to the press or even a legal society or union attracts the suspicious attention of his superiors. In this respect, his freedom is even more limited than that of the ordinary Russian citizen, who is restricted enough.[1]

Concerning potential dangers of education, liberals and officials shared common assumptions from which, however, they drew very different conclusions. Liberals enthusiastically supported education for the same reason that the autocracy feared it: the belief that its wide-spread dissemination would ultimately result in profound changes in the political, social, and economic fabric of the nation. Consequently they staunchly opposed those autocratic policies which stemmed from the fear of ideas and education: censorship, police surveillance of students, the differentiated school network, and discriminatory measures which made it more difficult for the underprivileged to attend the elite schools.

Although most liberals would not have denied Russia's great need for qualified individuals in numerous areas of work, they did not as a rule view the utility of education in pragmatic terms. They thought that the further development and expansion of the educational system was vital to the future of Russia not because it would produce trained personnel, but because it would produce harmoniously developed individuals capable of fulfilling the "high national purpose of awakening and renewing the country."[2]

When we come to the fourth and, with hindsight, perhaps the most questionable of the autocratic approaches to education, however, we find considerable agreement. That Russia's schools should be based on those Western models which emphasized the development of abstract intellectual skills was believed still more strongly by the Westernized intelligentsia than by the autocracy. True, there was widespread opposition to Tolstoi's classicism. But most opponents of the classical gymnasium objected to its elitist implications rather than its foreign origin, and argued for the establishment of a Prussian-type realschule with equal rights alongside the gymnasium rather than for the abandonment of foreign models with their strictly academic subjects. Very few followed Ushinskii (much less Karamzin!) when these individuals questioned the very practice of wholesale borrowing from the West. Russian liberals were thoroughly influenced by Western ideas, and it is not surprising that in several respects they went much further than the autocracy on this issue. Professors, for example, frequently complained that Russian universities were not sufficiently similar to their German prototypes. Liberals furthermore insisted that Westernized academic schools should be made available to the entire population, whereas the autocracy was inclined to restrict this kind of instruction only to the more prestigious of its schools.

To be sure, two important trends that emerged at this time bear witness to the fact that not all public or liberal figures believed unquestionably in the desirability of a strictly academic approach to education at all levels. One was a movement to promote vocational-technical education, which had some sponsors in the public sphere and which led to the establishment of networks in the Ministry of Education in the 1880s and in the Ministry of Finance in the 1890s. The other was the development after 1900 of a number of progressive pedagogical movements in Russia that were heavily influenced by the learn-through-doing and work-oriented theories of Western pedagogical thinkers such as John Dewey and George Kerschensteiner.[3] But most liberals remained suspicious of vocational education unless, as in the case of the system developed by Finance Minister Sergei Witte (Vitte), it was based on a solid general educational curriculum. And whereas the progressive pedagogues had a considerable impact on early Soviet educational thought and practice, the extent of their influence on contemporary Russian liberal thought may be questioned. When a progressive official in the Ministry of Agriculture, himself under the influence of Dewey, tried to introduce a more practical orientation in its schools, he encountered much opposition in the Duma, where the ministry was accused of trying to turn the schools into vocational schools and give them over to the specialists. Only the staunch support of peasant members in the Duma allowed the program to be carried through.[4]

The most succinct programmatic statement of liberal educational opinion is contained in the charter adopted by the All-Russian Union of Teachers at its founding congress in June 1905. Stressing the need for local autonomy, free and equal access to educational facilities, and general education rather than vocational training, the charter called for the following reforms:

a. the integration of the entire school network so that the general educational school at the secondary level will be a direct continuation of the primary school;

b. the introduction of universal, free, and compulsory primary education, and of free secondary and higher education;

c. the abolition of compulsory religious instruction;

d. the establishment of curricula featuring general education and freedom of teaching;

e. freedom to teach in the native tongue of the local population in all types of schools;

f. the transfer of responsibility for the administration of public education to organs of local self-government, elected on the basis of a universal (without discrimination concerning either sex or nationality), equal, direct, and secret ballot, and to social groups organized according to the principle of nationality.[5]

This all-too-brief survey of liberal attitudes toward education will be supplemented and substantiated by a more detailed examination of the liberal professoriate in Part Two. But for the present it is sufficient to suggest that the much vaunted irreconcilable differences in outlook between autocracy and liberals were not as pervasive as has commonly been presented by contemporaries and historians. That education in and of itself had tremendous potential to transform the institutions of a given country, and that the highly academic institutions of the West were the most appropriate models for Russian schools were two assumptions which were so taken for granted by a majority of both liberals and officials that mutual agreement on them was not even noticed.

It must not, of course, be denied that very substantial differences remained. The most important was the issue of autocratic control versus local autonomy. The Ministry of Education's frequently clumsy efforts to control local initiative invariably alienated public-spirited individuals, who were inclined to refer to it as the "Ministry for the Prevention of Public Education."[6] Nonetheless, despite mutual distrust, interminable delays, and bureaucratic red tape, there began to take place a strained cooperation that resulted in the emergence of a host of new educational institutions owing their origin to private individuals or public institutions (usually zemstvos or municipal dumas) rather than the central state apparatus. An examination of the size and character of the schools that emerged from this cooperation will enable us to assess more accurately the nature of the liberal impact on Russian education before the Revolution.

Primary education, the area of Russia's greatest need, was also the area in which the public received the least amount of scope for unfettered independent activity. Zemstvo educational expenditures rose steadily during this period, both in absolute terms and as a percentage of the total zemstvo budget.[7] As we shall see, however, the government was willing to utilize zemstvo efforts but not to relinquish administrative control over the schools themselves. Somewhat more leeway was granted to the establishment of public or private schools at the secondary and higher level. Furthermore, one suspects that it was at these levels that the typical urban liberal professional was most anxious to devote his energies.

The most important distinguishing feature among state, public, and private schools was the presence or absence of legal rights for the students. Throughout the nineteenth century, educational certification had both removed barriers and provided tangible benefits to graduates desiring to enter the civil service. In the first place, entry into the table of ranks was simply barred to most of those whose social estate was lower than that of merchant of the first guild, unless they were graduates of a state secondary or higher educational institution. It required a doctor's, master's, or medical degree to circumvent the prohibition against Jews entering the civil service, although a regular higher education diploma would at least free them from the necessity of living in the Pale of Settlement. Secondly, those with higher degrees were guaranteed entry at specified levels of the table of ranks: those with a doctor's degree at the eighth rank; those with a master's at the ninth; those with a higher educational honors' diploma at the tenth; those with a regular diploma at the twelfth; and those with a gymnasium honors' certificate at the fourteenth.[8]

Although there were some private and public schools which enjoyed all the same legal rights that accrued to the state schools, they had to be organized exactly as their state counterparts, with all the teaching appointments ratified by the ministry. A second category of schools had full legal rights for pupils (but not teachers), on condition that the pupils pass state examinations administered by a local ministry official. A final category of schools had no legal rights whatever, and although even they were subject to certain ministerial regulations, they had considerably more autonomy than the other schools.[9]

Frequently there was input from several different sources in the founding of these schools. A wealthy individual might make a large donation, a municipal duma would contribute a building or a piece of land, and the ministry, which would have to approve the project in any event (especially the proposed curriculum) might or might not contribute some of the operating expenses.

The greatest spurt in the founding of public and private schools occurred during 1905-08, a time when the nearly bankrupt government was hard pressed by oppositionist demands and the ministry was headed by relatively liberal ministers. Whereas there were 7 private boys' gymnasia before 1905, there were 67 by 1908 and 127 by 1911. By 1908 there were also 69 public gymnasia, supported by municipalities and zemstvos.[10]

But it was in the establishment of new types of educational institutions, rather than in the supplementing of the already existing network, that public initiative made its most important contribution. Women's educational institutions, which will be discussed below, form the best example of this type of effort. Another example was the "people's. university" (*narodnyi universitet*) movement, which sponsored public lectures for working adults. A number of private scientific societies sponsored research and scientific meetings. The Ledentsov Society for the Advancement of Exact Sciences was particularly helpful in granting funds to provide private laboratory space for many of the professors who resigned in the wake of the 1911 crisis at Moscow University.[11]

Advanced pedagogical research and education, long a neglected area in Russia, also benefited from private and public initiative. When a group of professors drew up a plan to establish pedagogical faculties at a number of universities, the ministry declined to supply the necessary funds. The Ministry of War proved more interested, and it was under its auspices that in 1904 the first systematic courses in child psychology were offered. By 1908 these courses had developed into the St. Petersburg Pedagogical Academy. In 1907 the Psychoneurological Institute was founded in St. Petersburg by V. M. Bekhterev, who was to play a prominent role in the psychological and pedagogical debates of Soviet Marxists in the 1920s and 1930s. In 1911 P. G. Shelaputin donated funds for a two-year pedagogical institute in Moscow.[12]

Mention should also be made of the only private municipal university in Russian history, founded by General A. L. Shaniavskii in 1908. It adopted an open admissions policy, maintained a flexible curriculum, and employed some of the leading professors of Moscow, including many who fled Moscow Universty in 1911. In short, Shaniavskii University, together with the women's higher courses and many other fruits of private initiative, helped to provide a certain amount of variety and flexibility in an otherwise heavily structured and authoritarian educational system.[13]

It is time now to turn in more detail to the development of women's education, which also witnessed tremendous expansion during the last twenty years of the empire. Although the autocracy had provided the original initiative in this area, the government in general and the Ministry of Education in particular were highly ambivalent toward women's education in the second half of the nineteenth century. The main impetus for its development came from private donors, dedicated individuals, and liberal public opinion.

Secondary education for girls was initiated by Catherine the Great, who founded the Smolnyi Institute as a boarding school for young ladies.[14] Sister schools were subsequently established, and in 1828 Empress Dowager Marie consolidated the system under her own jurisdiction as Section IV of His Majesty's Special Chancery (generally known as the Administration of Empress Marie). In 1858 the administration established an additional system of day gymnasia for girls. Both the day gymnasia and the more genteel boarding schools continued to exist under the Administration of Empress Marie until the Revolution, but in 1911 they enrolled a total of only 25,620 pupils.[15]

Approximately equal in size was the girls' secondary school network operated by the Holy Synod. Designed primarily for daughters of the clergy who intended to become primary school teachers, these schools enrolled some 21,000 pupils in 1912.[16]

By the turn of the century, however, both of these networks had been exceeded in size and importance by a burgeoning system of girls' gymnasia that was controlled but not funded by the Ministry of Education. Municipalities and private individuals took the initiative in founding these schools, which depended largely on tuition for income. Thus, in 1899 only 9 percent of their total budget came from the central state apparatus. Nonetheless, the ministry kept a careful watch on the schools and insisted that they conform to its regulations. They were not required, however, to offer the same heavily classical curriculum as the boys' gymnasia, and there were significant differences in curriculum from one school to another. Teachers' salaries in the girls' schools were much lower — perhaps a half or even a quarter — than those paid in the state-supported boys' gymnasia. Although this fact may have had a deleterious impact on the quality of education provided, the relative cheapness of founding girls' schools compared to boys' may help to explain the dramatic growth of the girls' gymnasia. Enrollments increased as follows:

| | |
|------|---------|
| 1873 | 23,000 |
| 1883 | 55,100 |
| 1893 | 65,500 |
| 1903 | 137,000 |
| 1913 | 303,700 |

In 1913–14 the combined enrollment of boys' gymnasia and realschulen was only 232,900. Thus the surprising fact emerges that on the eve of World War I the general secondary schools of the empire were educating considerably more girls than boys.[17]

Equally important was the expansion of higher educational facilities for women during this period. The right to obtain a higher education was the leading goal of the women's movement in Russia during the late nineteenth and early twentieth centuries. By 1914 this movement had achieved considerable success but still had not reached the goal of educational equality.

Although during the post-Crimean thaw several universities authorized women to attend lectures as auditors, this practice was forbidden upon the introduction of the new university charter of 1863.

Except for the brief period of 1906–08, women were to be barred from attending universities and virtually all other men's higher educational institutions until the onset of World War I.

The initial reaction of a small but determined contingent of Russian women was to seek a university education abroad. Other European universities were also closed to women at this time (although a few permitted female auditors), but the persistent efforts of a Russian student, N. P. Suslova, produced a breach in this policy at the University of Zurich. In 1867 she successfully petitioned to become the first woman regularly admitted to a university on an equal basis with men, and subsequently received her medical degree. Other women followed Suslova's lead, with by far the largest national contingent coming from Russia. In 1872, 60 out of the 67 female students at the University of Zurich were Russians, and a sizeable radical colony of both male and female Russian émigrés had developed in Zurich.[18] The possibility of Russian women imbibing revolutionary ideas while studying abroad began to alarm tsarist officials, who thereupon reluctantly granted permission for the organization of women's higher educational facilities in Russia.

A petition for permission to organize women's courses signed by close to four hundred women was presented to St. Petersburg University and Education Minister Tolstoi in 1868. The university responded quite favorably. A number of professors, including the world famous scientists D. I. Mendeleev and I. M. Sechenov, volunteered to give lectures for no salary during the first year. Tolstoi responded more warily, insisting that the project be limited to the organization of public lectures, open to both sexes. As a result, the Petersburg (later Vladimirskie) Public Courses came into being, with a first year registration of over 900 students, the overwhelming majority of whom were women. A similar development occurred in Moscow. A group of women requested V. I. Guerrier (Ger'e), professor of history at Moscow University, to help them establish women's courses. The ministry granted permission, and in 1872 the Guerrier Courses, as they were popularly called, began operation. Specializing in the humanities, the courses had among their faculty such intellectual luminaries as the historian V. O. Kliuchevskii, the philosopher Vladimir Soloviev (Solov'ev), and the economist A. I. Chuprov. A separate institution, the Lubianskie Courses, offered instruction to women in the sciences.[19]

New impetus was given to the movement by an 1876 decree which explicitly authorized the establishment of women's courses in all the university cities of the empire. Courses were opened soon thereafter in Kazan and Kiev. Founders of the Vladimirskie Public Courses in St.

Petersburg took advantage of the decree to reorganize their lecture series into a regular school, thereafter called the Bestuzhev Higher Courses for Women. Applicants for admission had to possess a secondary school certificate and pay tuition of fifty rubles per year. The school received only a small grant from the government but was so successful in raising private donations that during 1879–85 its income exceeded expenditures. It had two faculties, historical-philological and physical-mathematical, both of which were staffed by moonlighting professors from St. Petersburg University and other local higher educational institutions.[20] The intention in this, as in other subsequent women's higher courses, was to offer an education similar in nature and academic standards to that of the men's universities.

Medical education for women was also launched during this period. After the Ministry of Education refused to approve a project for independent medical courses for women, War Minister Miliutin expressed interest in the idea. As a result, separate women's courses were attached to the army's Medical-Surgical Academy, where they functioned from 1872 to the mid-80s.[21]

The movement for women's education received a severe setback in the 1880s, when Pobedonostsev and Delianov assumed control of Russia's educational destinies. Considerable official disagreement on the issue resulted in a Delianov decree of 1886 which ordered the gradual closure of all existing women's courses pending the publication by the government of a new uniform set of rules and regulations. The official commission appointed to draw up the regulations proved unable to agree, and consequently in 1889 all the schools but one were closed. The single exception was the Bestuzhev Courses, which were permitted to continue on a restricted basis.[22]

At the end of the 1890s, however, the government again began to authorize private groups to establish women's higher courses. The Medical Institute for Women opened its doors in St. Petersburg in 1897, and the Moscow Courses of Higher Education for Women began instruction in 1900. In 1905 the Ministry of Education gave permission for thirty such schools to be established, and by 1910 twenty schools in eleven cities were already functioning. They offered education in both general and professional fields. Medical training was especially in demand. The courses in Moscow, St. Petersburg, Kiev, Kharkov, Iuriev, and Odessa all had medical faculties, whereas separate medical schools for women were founded in Moscow in 1909 and Kharkov in 1910.[23]

A final major breakthrough was a 1911 law which permitted graduates of the women's higher courses to take the state administered university examinations and granted to successful candidates the same rights that accrued to university graduates.[24] Women, however, were still not admitted to the men's universities, a slight exception to this rule being made only under the unusual circumstances of World War I.

The tremendous quantitative significance of this drive for women's higher education can be judged from the fact that by 1914-15 enrollment in the women's higher courses, most of which had developed only in the last decade and half, was almost equal to the enrollment of the century-old universities and constituted 30 percent of the students in all types of higher educational institutions of the empire.[25]

It is appropriate now to pause in order to make a partial evaluation of the liberal impact on the educational system during the decade and a half before Russia was plunged into war and revolution. One can only be impressed by the tremendous energy and zeal with which public-spirited individuals approached their self-appointed tasks, and with the amazing quantitative results they achieved in the face of so many obstacles. It is undeniable that many of the schools they founded or initiated provided a highly prized education to groups that would have been otherwise excluded, and in some cases offered an alternative type of educational institution which increased the flexibility and freedom of choice within the entire network. Yet when one views the liberal approach in the context of the educational needs of the country as a whole, some debits must be noted. The liberal educational effort, important as it was, was focused not where Russian education was weakest, but where it was strongest: urban secondary and higher educational institutions offering Westernized academic curricula.[26] The main sponsors of the public and private institutions came from the professional middle class, which did not have close ties with the industrialists and was not attuned to the manpower needs of an industrializing society, but which retained instead an educational preference for the liberal arts and traditional professions. Such individuals were generally aware of the great need to bridge the gap between the educated few in the cities and illiterate masses in the countryside. But their efforts to close this gap by the expansion of secondary and higher educational institutions designed to develop abstract intellectual skills rather than by lower-level schools that would employ a more practical methodology can, in retrospect, only be regarded as highly unrealistic.

## THE AUTOCRACY UNDER PRESSURE

State education planners found themselves buffeted from four different sources during this period. There were the omnipresent conservative pressures to retain intact traditional practices, no matter how inconsistent or ineffective they had proven. There were the spiraling series of student demonstrations, strikes, demands, and turmoil. There was constant pressure from the liberal public to reform the state institutions in its own image. Finally, both the internal industrialization program and international military pressures underscored the need for rapid educational change and innovation.

To say that no overall strategy was conceived to cope with these pressures would be a great understatement. The fact that during the last twenty years there were ten different ministers of education in itself bears eloquent witness to the striking lack of continuity that occurred. A brief chronological survey will make the point still more clearly. Delianov's successors, N. P. Bogolepov (1898-1901) and General P. S. Vannovskii (1901-2), were unpopular figures, but both implemented measures which loosened up the Tolstoi system, and Vannovskii drafted projects that would have entailed much more extensive changes. But in the repetition of a familiar cycle, the assassination of Minister of Interior D. S. Sipiagin in 1902 forced the resignation of Vannovskii and the shelving of his reform projects. A somewhat harder line was maintained until the upsurge of 1905 coerced the autocracy to make a number of important concessions in the educational as well as political sphere. Most of these concessions, however, were subsequently withdrawn, as Ministers A. N. Schwartz (Shvarts) (1908-10) and L. N. Kasso (1910-14) desperately tried to reassert autocratic control over a rapidly growing and increasingly complex educational system. As a final inconsistency, we find perhaps the most intelligent and far-sighted of all Russia's education ministers, P. N. Ignatiev, occupying the post during the heyday of Rasputin, 1915-16.

Rather than to continue in chronological terms, it will be more appropriate to examine separately the various sectors of the educational system in order to ascertain the nature of the changes that did and did not occur between 1900 and World War I. The most noteworthy event in the area of primary education was a 1908 agreement between the autocracy and the Duma to a law which called for the gradual introduction of compulsory, free, four-year education for all children between the ages of eight and eleven. The central government allocated considerable funds for the project, which envisioned 1922 as the target year when universal primary school attendance would be achieved in practice.[27] The staggering size of the task involved, however, can be judged from the fact that despite a 67 percent increase in primary enrollments between 1905 and 1914, almost half of all eight- to eleven-year-olds remained outside the school system as Russia entered World War I.[28]

But whereas governmental conservatives were willing to endorse the rapid expansion of primary schools, they refused to countenance a Duma plan to overhaul and decentralize the administrative structure of the primary system. The conservative State Council rejected in 1911 a Duma bill that would have absorbed all church schools into the secular network, transferred from the ministry to the zemstvos and municipal dumas prime responsibility for supervising the schools, and permitted the use of local languages in non-Russian areas. The separate primary network of the Holy Synod, although it stopped growing after 1905, continued to exist until 1917. Education Minister Kasso tried to reassert strict ministerial control over curriculum and teaching staff and to restrict the application of 1906-7 measures that permitted teaching in non-Russian languages.[29] The belated spurt in primary education thus occurred within the traditional context of centralized autocratic controls.

A few changes were made in secondary school policy. Foes of classicism were gratified by a reduction in the number of hours of Latin and a reduction or (in many gymnasia) even elimination of Greek. Increased curricular emphasis was now placed on Russian language, literature, geography, and history. This change meant that for the first time in thirty years incoming university students would have had some prior systematic study of their native land. The ministry also encouraged a less formal classroom atmosphere, and during the 1905 upheaval it authorized the formation of parents' committees. But if its classicism had been diluted and its administration somewhat liberalized, the Tolstoi gymnasium in 1914 still bore most of the essential marks of its origin. Vannovskii's recommendation that gymnasia and realschulen be merged into a single type had been shelved by his successor, and the gymnasium continued to retain its privileged position vis-à-vis the realschule. Latin remained its curricular staple, strict surveillance was maintained over its pupils, and the maturity examination only it could grant continued to be a virtual prerequisite for university admission.[30]

But whereas dogged ministerial determination resisted liberal demands for more extensive and badly needed changes in gymnasium structure, it was the liberals who opposed beneficial reform projects put forth by the bureaucracy in the course of the prolonged debate over reform of the six-year municipal school. These schools, which were located not only in cities but also in suburbs and villages, had been designed to provide an education beyond that of the primary school for pupils of modest means and social origin. Relatively inexpensive for the state to administer, they could have played a major role in furnishing some education for hundreds of thousands of youths who, either because of lack of aptitude or remoteness of location, were unlikely to attend the more costly and demanding realschulen or gymnasia. Yet instead of forming a broader educational base below the realschulen and gymnasia, they actually had a smaller enrollment than the more academic schools. In 1905 there were in the entire empire 729 municipal schools with 113,415 pupils, compared to approximately 102,000 gymnasium and 47,000 realschule pupils.[31]

The need to reform the municipal schools was clear to all. In 1901 the ministry unveiled a plan which, among other things, would have given the schools a more vocational orientation. Russia's need for this type of school should have been obvious. The ministry's vocational network founded in 1888 had failed to expand rapidly, and as late as 1912 there were only three middle-level vocational schools for the entire industrialized area of St. Petersburg.

This and subsequent proposals, however, were opposed by teachers and liberal Duma members who insisted that the main object of the reform should be not to vocationalize the schools but to strengthen their general educational character and convert them into stepping stones to the realschulen and gymnasia. Due to the widespread disagreement, nothing was done until 1912, when a compromise measure was implemented which called for the conversion of the municipal schools into four-year "upper primary schools."[32]

Russian universities experienced both deep crisis and continued growth during this period. The crisis stemmed from the merging of the traditional current of student activism with the revolutionary movements of 1905. In August of that year the autocracy granted the concession of substantial university autonomy, following which students and others, despite professorial protests, used higher educational facilities as a center for mass revolutionary agitation that culminated in the general strike of October of that year. The autocracy neither forgot nor forgave this role. Universities were among the main victims of the reaction that began in 1907, as Education Ministers Schwartz and Kasso zealously sought to restrict or withdraw the concessions that had been made under pressure during the revolutionary period. The nadir in ministry-university relations occurred in 1910–11, when Kasso ordered police onto the campus of Moscow University to break up student meetings. The upshot of the incident was the dismissal of the rector and two deans, followed by the resignation in protest of over one hundred faculty members—including the core of Russia's scientific and scholarly elite.[33] Meanwhile, high-placed officials began to question the wisdom of continued university expansion. Although approval was given for the opening of a new university at Saratov in 1909, Nicholas II reflected widespread feeling in the Council of Ministers when in 1912 he stipulated that Russia had enough universities and should concentrate instead on establishing new institutes at the secondary and higher educational levels. All of these actions greatly alarmed the liberal professoriate, which regarded them as the final abandonment of the government's commitment to maintain a strong university system based predominantly on the German model.[34]

Nonetheless, universities shared in the general enrollment boom of all educational institutions at this time. Indeed, in the brief period between 1904 and 1908 most universities witnessed a virtual doubling in the size of their enrollments, a growth which was only partially caused by an abnormal bunching of students due to the closure of the universities during 1905-6.[35] A peak of 38,600 students was reached in 1909, after which admission restrictions led to a slight decrease. By 1913 total university enrollment was 35,700, which represented a more than 100 percent increase over 1900.[36]

Despite the revolutionary turmoil, the highly antagonistic behavior of the ministry, and the increased call by many scientists for the establishment of private research institutes, Russian universities before the war continued to perform their function of high-level teaching and research in most of the important disciplines of Western learning. After 1905, increased emphasis was placed on student research in the form of "practical activities" (*prakticheskie zaniatiia*) such as laboratory work and small seminars.[37] The universities overtook the Academy of Sciences as the source of the most innovative research. In the words of one authority, "The universities became the true center of the national effort in science; and in learned societies, government science bureaus, and the Academy of Sciences the most prominent members were always professors."[38]

The universities, then, as well as the ministry's secondary and primary schools, were handling greatly expanded enrollments with little or no change in either their basic tasks and functions or in their administrative structure. What about funding? Were the three sectors receiving the necessary budgetary allotments to enable them both to keep pace with inflation and enrollments and to carry out their assigned tasks?

Higher education officials were quick to complain that they were not. An official of the St. Petersburg Technological Institute stated that the Ministry of Education's stinginess prevented the school from becoming as well equipped as similar institutes in Europe and the United States.[39] D. I. Bagalei, a professor and former university rector who sat on the State Council, argued in 1914 that state funds for university teaching positions and salaries had increased by an average of only 57 percent since 1884, and that capital allocations for building purposes were also woefully inadequate. He chastised the ministry for foot-dragging and for introducing only palliative measures with regard to university finance.[40]

An overview of the entire budget of the Ministry of Education suggests, however, that while higher education benefited considerably less than other sectors, the ministry was nonetheless pouring greatly increased funds into education at all levels. For example, in absolute terms the ministry's budget increased by nearly four times during the period 1902–13.[41] More importantly, the ministry's share of the total state budget increased significantly. From 1866 to 1909 this percentage had fluctuated between 1.5 and 2.5, but by 1914 it had climbed to 4.4 percent.[42] The lion's share of the increase went to the drive to achieve compulsory primary education. Between 1907 and 1912 the proportion of the ministry's budget devoted to primary education jumped from 20 percent to 40 percent, while the amount spent on secondary schools, though doubling in absolute terms, declined from 30 percent to 21 percent.[43] Although the universities might well claim that they were getting short-changed in the process, the ministry was finally taking definite measures to reverse the long-standing expenditures bias in favor of the higher and secondary sectors at the expense of the primary. This reallocation of budgetary priorities in favor of primary education was the single most important and beneficial policy change conducted by the Ministry of Education during the reign of Nicholas II.

But while the Ministry of Education was finally implementing a few obviously needed and long overdue changes, it was another state organ, the Ministry of Finance, that had the imagination and foresight to create totally new educational institutions that were ideally suited to the Russian environment. Having lost their vocational-technical schools to the jurisdiction of the Ministry of Public Education in 1881, Finance Ministers Vyshnegradskii (1887–92) and Witte (1892–1903) decided to establish a new educational network that would be oriented to the commercial and industrial needs of the country, and more flexible in its educational approach than the schools of the Ministry of Education. (In 1905 this network was transferred from the Ministry of Finance to the newly created Ministry of Trade and Industry, but it continued to be operated on the same principles.)

A statute of 1896 called for the establishment of short-term trade and commercial courses for working adults, three-year trade schools, and, most importantly, a system of commercial schools offering a seven- to eight-year course of instruction. Schools could be founded by the government, local authorities, or private individuals and groups, and considerable local autonomy was granted in the administration of the schools. The Finance Ministry published a model curriculum for the commercial schools, but its implementation was not binding. Despite their overtly vocational character, the commercial schools were noted for their stress on general educational subjects and for that reason began to rival the gymnasia and realschulen in public esteem. Many experienced teachers, tired of the bureaucratic formalism of the Ministry of Education, were happy to switch to new positions in the commercial schools. Other reasons for their popularity included the limited introduction of coeducation in 1905, and the fact that Jewish quotas did not apply. Starting from a level of 3,000 pupils in 1895, enrollment grew to 51,632 in 1913-14—compared to 80,800 in realschulen and 152,100 in boys' gymnasia at that time.[44]

The Finance Ministry made equally important contributions to the development of higher education. It opened a new commercial institute in Moscow in 1906, and between 1907 and 1914 higher commercial education became the fastest growing sector in higher education enrollments.[45]

Still more important, and Witte's proudest educational accomplishment, was the establishment of completely new polytechnical institutes in Kiev and Warsaw (1898) and St. Petersburg (1902). These well-endowed institutes helped to initiate systematic scholarly analysis of technological development in the broad context of general economic growth, an intellectual approach that eventually spread to some of the country's older technological institutes and which helped lay much of the groundwork for the central economic planning that was subsequently adopted by the Bolsheviks.[46]

It was not without difficulty, however, that Witte secured approval for the founding of the St. Petersburg Polytechnical Institute. The potential advantages of new higher educational institutions were not readily apparent to many governmental figures at a time when demonstrations and strikes by university students were sweeping the country. To calm such fears, Witte decided to locate his institute in an isolated district (Sosnovka) far from the center of the city and, it was hoped, safe from the revolutionary contamination of other students. (Nonetheless, the institute and its students fully participated in the revolutionary disturbances of 1905-7.) He lavished eight million rubles on its construction ("truly a monstrous sum," in the words of Nicholas II), thereby making it the best equipped higher school in Russia at that time.[47]

One of the innovative features of the new institute was its independent faculty of economics (which enrolled approximately half of the student body) in addition to the more typical technical faculties of metallurgy, electromechanics, and ship-building. The teaching staff included not only famous scientists such as N. A. Menshutkin, but also controversial intellectual figures such as economists Peter Struve and M. I. Tugan-Baranovskii, who were barred from teaching at the regular universities because of their political views. Most teachers were interested in practical applications as well as theory, emphasizing laboratory work and discussion groups rather than lectures. Memoirs testify to close teacher-student relations and to an esprit de corps unusual for educational institutions at that time.[48]

In conclusion, our evaluation of the efforts of the state educational authorities during this period must be similar to our view of the liberal contribution: mixed, but weighted toward the negative. There were some bright spots, in particular the innovative schools established by the Ministry of Finance and the ability of the Ministry of Education to increase its total budget and to allocate a much larger percentage of it to the primary sector. Yet traditional practices and long-standing policy contradictions remained all too evident. The actions of Education Ministers Schwartz (1908-10) and Kasso (1910-14) afford ample evidence that, whatever concessions to public initiative had been made during the revolution of 1905, the bureaucracy continued to regard local autonomy with the greatest suspicion. The government continued to fear the effects of education, yet felt compelled to increase expenditures on educational expansion. The bureaucracy wanted to control and firmly guide the educational process, yet jurisdiction over various schools remained divided among several ministries having different outlooks and different priorities. The autocracy staked its existence on the support of the landed nobility, yet its program of educational expansion benefited primarily the city-dwellers and led to a steady diminution of gentry representation in schools and universities. The empire required skilled individuals for posts in the government and the economy, yet its education officials generally failed to inquire whether the European academic curricula of Russian schools were providing the type of training that was most urgently needed.

But if most of the traditional characteristics of Russian education remained intact by 1914, during the course of World War I there appeared a Minister of Education who was willing to change them. Count Paul N. Ignatiev, who served from January 1915 to December 1916, may well have been "the best Minister of Education that Russia ever had."[49] Yet this able official, whose task would have been difficult enough in any period, had the misfortune of coming into office at the worst possible time: when the financial strains of the war in and of themselves were sufficient to prevent the full implementation of his programs, and when the desperate malaise afflicting the ruling circles

of the autocracy was reaching its climax. Indeed, it was at the behest of
the Rasputin clique that Ignatiev was eventually removed from office by
Nicholas II, just two months before the autocracy itself crumbled into
dust.

The significance of Ignatiev's approach to educational reform lay in
his willingness to break with two long-standing traditions: the autocratic distrust of public educational initiative, and the autocratic-
liberal affinity for highly abstract and intellectual curricula. Soon after
taking office, he jolted the curators of the educational districts by
insisting that they listen to and take into account public wishes concerning educational policy. He himself actively sought public input
while drawing up his draft reforms, a fact which in itself made him
extremely popular in public if not bureaucratic circles.[50]

His attitude toward curricular reform, however, attacked one of the
deeply held axioms of the liberal intelligentsia. As an official in the
Ministry of Agriculture, he had earlier tried to orient some of the
peasant schools in a more pragmatic direction. He subsequently received a copy of Dewey's *School and Society*, which he found to be
completely in accord with his own convictions.[51] He thereupon aligned
himself with the small but growing progressive pedagogical movement
in Russia, which diagnosed Russia's educational backwardness as stemming not merely from the insufficient number of primary schools, but
also from the "scholastic" nature of the education provided by the
existing schools. Ignatiev criticized the existing system of education in
the following terms:

> Its detachment from the actualities of life and from the
> practical interests of the people, its tendency to develop a pro-
> pensity for abstract thought rather than the realities of ordi-
> nary life made people in general lukewarm to it, and the
> peasantry regarded it with no confidence whatever. I recall the
> words of a peasant member of one of the zemstvos: "If you are
> going to multiply the sort of schools you have now," he said,
> "you will be able to get all the clerks you want for fifty copecks
> a day. But three rubles won't get you a single laborer." The
> secondary schools were filled with the same zest for abstraction.
> More than that, in their courses there was nothing that was
> rounded out and conclusive, for their sole aim was to prepare
> matriculants for the universities. But only a minority of high-
> school students went on to the universities. The rest were
> launched into the realities of life without any training that was
> really basic, and wholly unprepared for whatever work might
> be awaiting them. Practical knowledge was held to be knowl-
> edge of an inferior order. The view of the human mind which

was held by the schools led them to ignore, or at any rate to underestimate, everything but the capacity of the pupil for abstract thinking, and to leave the other sides of his nature untrained and undeveloped. There is only one educational system that can meet the needs of life, satisfy the demands of the people, and at the same time fulfil the dictates of education in every sense of the word. That is a school system which can minister equally to every phase of our human desire to acquire knowledge — knowledge that is concrete and practical as well as abstract — and look without bias upon all human achievements.[52]

Ignatiev's specific proposals for secondary school reform would have created a ladder system by transforming the existing gymnasia and realschulen into a single type of seven-year school that would be directly attached to the primary network, and that in its senior years would be subdivided into classical, modern language, and natural science divisions. Each subdivision would offer an education that would be complete in itself, but would also permit the graduate to go on to university or other higher education.[53] Concerning higher education, he was well aware of the contradiction between expecting the universities to devote themselves to scientific research and the furthering of knowledge on the one hand, and expecting them to train qualified specialists for practical work on the other hand. His proposed solution was to make a more explicit division between the two tasks. His draft university charter granted extensive autonomy to the universities and stipulated research to be their main responsibility. Simultaneously, however, he called for both expansion and increased government control over the country's professional and technical institutes, the main function of which would be to train specialists needed by the government and the economy.[54] In order to coordinate the important task of planning and administering the country's specialized educational institutions, he established the Council for Matters Relating to Vocational Education, composed of representatives of several different ministries and industrial concerns.[55] Although Ignatiev pressed for the rapid implementation of compulsory primary education, he did not perceive a resource imbalance between the higher and primary sectors, and in fact called for vigorous expansion of the higher education network as well.[56]

Owing to the war and the deteriorating political situation, Ignatiev was able to implement only a minor fraction of his reform projects. Although many of his ideas were subsequently adopted by the Provisional Government and the Bolsheviks, they had no significant impact on Russian society before the February Revolution. Even had his term of office occurred in less tumultuous times, there is no assurance that he would have been able to muster the political strength necessary to get his program accepted. His role was that of a diagnostician, rather than healer, of tsarist Russia's educational ailments.

PLUS ÇA CHANGE. . .

An examination of selected Russian and international education statistics will serve to supplement and confirm many of the preceding judgments. We shall be most interested in data which will both indicate the extent of change in the Russian educational structure during the last two decades before the Revolution, and provide a comparison with the educational structures of other countries.

The most astonishing discovery is that despite the vast increase in funds poured into the primary system, Russia's long-standing disproportionately high enrollments in secondary and higher educational institutions actually intensified during this period. Table 1 shows the trends in Russia's enrollment structure that occurred throughout the nineteenth and early twentieth centuries.

TABLE 1

Ratios of Primary, Secondary, and Higher Educational
Students between 1801 and 1914

| Year | Students at all levels as % of population | Secondary pupils per 1000 primary pupils | Higher-education students per 1000 primary pupils |
| --- | --- | --- | --- |
| 1801 | .1 | 92 | 9 |
| 1825 | .4 | 113 | 21 |
| 1835 | .4 | 106 | 14 |
| 1845 | .5 | 89 | 12 |
| 1855 | .6 | 72 | 16 |
| 1865 | 1.1 | 61 | 9 |
| 1875 | 1.3 | 93 | 9 |
| 1885 | 1.7 | 93 | 9 |
| 1895 | 2.3 | 63 | 6 |
| 1905 | 3.9 | 67 | 10 |
| 1914 | 5.5 | 72 | 15 |

SOURCE: Adapted from Michael Kaser, "Education in Tsarist and Soviet Development," in C. Abramsky, ed., *Essays in Honour of E. H. Carr* (London, 1974), p. 235.

If an effective crash campaign to reduce social disparities by increasing the availability of primary education had in fact been put into effect during the last years of tsardom, then we would expect the ratio of the number of secondary and higher-education students to the number of primary pupils to have diminished. There would have been a broadening of the base of the pyramid representing those currently enrolled in all schools, a larger and larger number of primary school pupils compared to those engaged in more advanced study. In fact, table 1 shows that the ratio of higher-education students to primary pupils was lowest during the Tolstoi and Pobedonostsev periods (although, as we shall see, it was still high even then by international standards), and that it actually began to climb sharply again after 1895. Despite the much-heralded zemstvo and Duma interest in educating the peasantry, therefore, it is clear that the secondary and higher-educational sectors, due largely to private-public efforts, were growing much more rapidly than the primary in the years before the war. Although increasing numbers of people were being educated, the traditional Russian tendency to emphasize advanced rather than elementary schooling was being perpetuated if not intensified.

No other major nineteenth-century European country had such high ratios of higher-secondary to primary enrollments.[57] A few international comparisons will serve to highlight the uniqueness of the tsarist educational structure, We shall start with illiteracy. As table 2 shows, Russia, despite a distinct advance since 1897, remained far and away the most illiterate of the major European powers. The only European countries with comparable rates were Bulgaria, Portugal, Rumania, Serbia, and Spain.

TABLE 2
Comparison of National Illiteracy Rates
before World War I

| Country | % Illiterate | Basis | Year |
| --- | --- | --- | --- |
| Russia | 70.0 | Pop. over 10 yrs. | 1897 |
| Russia | 61-62 | Pop. over 8 yrs. | 1913 |
| Italy | 48.2 | Pop. over 10 yrs. | 1901 |
| Hungary | 40.9 | Pop. over 12 yrs. | 1900 |
| Austria | 26.2 | Pop. over 10 yrs. | 1900 |
| Gt. Britain | 13.5 | Army recruits | 1907 |
| Belgium | 18.6 | Pop. over 10 yrs. | 1900 |
| France | 14.1 | Pop. over 10 yrs. | 1906 |
| U.S.A. | 7.7 | Pop. over 10 yrs. | 1910 |
| Germany | .03 | Army recruits | 1905 |

SOURCE: For Russia (1913), A. Rashin, "Gramotnost' i narodnoe obrazovanie v Rossii v XIX i nachale XX v." [Literacy and public education in Russia in the 19th and beginning of the 20th centuries], *Istoricheskie zapiskie* [Historical notes], 37 (1951): 28–50. For all others, Paul Monroe, ed., *A Cyclopedia of Education*, 5 vols. (New York, 1911–12), 3:383.

Russia's low national rate of literacy was closely correlated to her low degree of urbanization. Table 3 presents a comparison of European rates of urbanization compiled by tsarist statisticians.

But if education and change developed only slowly in the village, they spread quite rapidly among the small sector of the population that lived in the cities. The Russian urban literacy rate was relatively high, especially in the capital cities of St. Petersburg and Moscow. In 1910 the total St. Petersburg literacy rate for those over six years of age was 76 percent (compared to somewhat less than 38 percent for the nation as a whole); for men alone it was 86 percent, and for males aged eleven through fifteen it was 95 percent. The Moscow figures were about 5 percent lower in each category. Petersburg and Moscow still trailed behind most European cities in terms of literacy, but not nearly to the same extent that Russia as a whole trailed other countries.[58] Two conclusions may be drawn from this fact. First, it confirms that urban life in Russia was changing dramatically in the decades preceding the war, and that most factory workers were receiving some education, either within or without the confines of the regular school system.

TABLE 3
Comparison of National Rates of Urbanization in 1914

| Country | % of Pop. Living in Cities |
|---------|----------------------------|
| England | 78 |
| Norway | 72 |
| Germany | 56.1 |
| U.S.A. | 41.5 |
| France | 41.2 |
| Italy | 26.4 |
| Hungary | 18.8 |
| Russia | 15 |

SOURCE: Tsentral'nyi statisticheskii komitet [Central statistical committee], *Statisticheskii ezhegodnik Rossii, 1914* [Statistical annual for Russia, 1914] (Petrograd, 1915), p. 61.

Secondly, however, it suggests that in terms of education and literacy (not to mention economic development), urban change was occurring at a much faster rate than rural change—which means that the unusually sharp cultural differences between city and countryside in Russia, so prevalent since the eighteenth century, were actually intensifying rather than diminishing during this period. The Russian city, its economy becoming industrialized and its inhabitants increasingly educated, was leaving the Russian village farther and farther behind on the road to modernization. By contributing to this differential rate of urban and rural change, educational policies, far from acting to bridge the gap between city-dweller and peasant, were actually helping to widen it.

A look at book publication statistics and higher education enrollments, in comparison with the national illiteracy rates, further highlights the huge cultural contrasts of late Imperial Russia. In 1913 Russia, despite her extensive illiteracy, was the second largest producer of books in the world, ranking close to Germany in number of titles, and equaling the total of France, the United States, and Great Britain combined.[59] Statistics on national higher education enrollments are not as complete or reliable as one would like, but table 4 furnishes convincing evidence of Russia's high position in this respect. To be sure, Russia's large total population was an important contributing factor to her high enrollment. When the figure is calculated as a ratio of students to population, Russia's international position is not so high. Unlike her national literacy rate, however, it still remains very close to those of other major powers.[60]

TABLE 4

Comparison of National Higher Educational Enrollments
before World War I

| Country | Higher educational enrollment | Year |
|---------|-------------------------------|------|
| U.S.A. | 355,000 | 1910 |
| Russia | 117,000 | 1913 |
| Germany | 77,000 | 1913 |
| United Kingdom | 71,000 | 1913 |
| France | 41,000 | 1910 |
| Italy | 28,000 | 1913 |
| Austria | 18,000 | 1913 |
| Hungary | 18,000 | 1913 |

SOURCES: For United Kingdom, computed from data in *Minerva: Jahrbuch der Gelehrten Welt*, vol. 23, 1913-14 (Strassburg, 1914). For all others, Joseph Ben-David, "The Growth of the Professions and the Class System," in Reinhard Bendix and Seymour M. Lipset, eds., *Class, Status and Power*, 2d ed. (New York, 1966), p. 463.

This general picture of an educational system very well developed at the upper levels but restricted to an unusually small sector of the population is further illustrated by recent calculations by Michael Kaser which compare Russia's educational structure with that of other countries at a comparable stage of economic development. Having calculated that Russia achieved a GNP of $200 per capita by about 1900, Japan in 1890, and Sweden 1880, Kaser presented the data shown in table 5, which demonstrate large divergencies in educational structure among the three countries. Thus, even though Russia's higher-secondary to primary ratios in 1900 were about the lowest for the entire century, and even though her total percentage of students had been increasing rapidly, her differences with both Japan and Sweden were nonetheless extraordinary.

One might finally inquire whether important changes occurred in the types of specialities offered by the burgeoning higher educational system. Table 6, however, indicates that enrollment shifts among various

TABLE 5

Comparison of Educational Structure of Countries
Having Comparable GNP Per Capita

| Country | % of population in all schools | Secondary pupils per 1000 primary pupils | Higher-education students per 1000 primary pupils |
|---|---|---|---|
| Russia (1900) | 3.5 | 65 | 8 |
| Japan (1890) | 8 | 9 | 4 |
| Sweden (1880) | 15 | 23 | 4 |

SOURCE: Adapted from data presented in Kaser, *Essays*, p. 243.

TABLE 6

Enrollment Shifts among Types of Higher Educational
Institutions between 1907 and 1914

| Type of higher education institution | Percentage of total enrollment | |
|---|---|---|
| | 1907 | 1914 |
| *Liberal arts and free professions* | | |
| General education (universities and women's higher courses with university-type programs) | 66.4 | 57.4 |
| Medical | 4.2 | 5.6 |
| Pedagogical | 2.5 | 3.1 |
| Juridical | 2.0 | 1.2 |
| Fine arts and music | 1.4 | 3.9 |
| Foreign languages | 1.2 | 0.8 |
| | 77.7 | 72.0 |
| *Technical-practical* | | |
| Agricultural | 2.6 | 2.7 |
| Technical | 18.8 | 18.1 |
| Commercial | .9 | 6.4 |
| | 22.3 | 27.2 |

SOURCE: L. K. Erman, "Sostav intelligentsii v Rossii v kontse XIX i nachale XX v." [The composition of the intelligentsia in Russia at the end of the 19th and the beginning of the 20th century], *Istoriia SSSR* [History of the USSR], no. 1 (1963), p. 172.

This table does not include data on the district of St. Petersburg. The "Medical" and "Juridical" categories refer only to the relatively few independent medical and juridical institutes. Most medical and legal training was conducted in the universities, and is reflected in the "General education" category.

specialties were rather limited during this period of rapid growth. Although it would be unwise to attach too much significance to the specific figures, owing to the absence of Petersburg data, we can none-theless treat with confidence the general trends reflected in the table. We find a slight drop in the liberal arts and professions, but this group in 1914 still represented well over two-thirds of the entire higher educa-tion enrollment. Witte's commercial institutes were the sole beneficiaries of the dip in general education. Significantly, both agricultural and technical institutes, though (like all categories) gaining in absolute terms during the period in question, failed to increase their proportionate share of total enrollments.

The foregoing analysis of autocratic approaches to education and of some of the statistical results of tsarist efforts has illuminated several aspects of what might be called the "external" side of Russian education. We have seen what the authorities at various times hoped to achieve by their educational programs, and the ways in which countervailing pressures led them to adopt policies that were basically inconsistent. A comparison of Russia's educational structure with that of other contemporary countries has confirmed that right up until 1917 the tsarist empire devoted an unusually small proportion of her total educational budget to primary schools in comparison with secondary and higher educational institutions. Reasons for this structural bias have been suggested — the centralizing tradition in Russian politics and the corresponding weakness of local administrative units; the affinity of both the autocracy and the liberal intelligentsia for advanced Western academic models; the authorities' awareness of the potential dangers of education and distrust of the liberal public. Whatever the reasons, however, the failure to give more adequate attention to the spread of primary education contributed to the sharp social divisions between the cities and the countryside, between the educated few and the unlearned masses.

It is time now to move from a discussion of autocratic attitudes and educational structure to an exploration of certain aspects of the internal history of Russian education. What went on within those schools which were the beneficiaries of imperial favor? How did those institutions which were based on foreign models adapt to their Russian environment? What role did they play in the development of Russian culture?

To pursue all of these questions to their fullest extent would take us far beyond the confines of the present volume. Accordingly, one particular group has been selected for special analysis. The Russian professoriate was the single most articulate and influential group of educators in tsarist Russia. While adhering to the main tenets of the liberal intelligentsia as a whole, members of the academic intelligentsia embraced in addition a distinctive outlook which stemmed directly from their view of their academic calling. This emergence of a specific professorial world view can be seen in retrospect as a natural if unanticipated by-product of the autocracy's decision to establish a Russian university system based on Western models. It is a perfect illustration of the rule that institutions borrowed from one country and implanted in another will tend to acquire significantly different characteristics in their new environment. In order to understand how this process took place, we must briefly retrace our steps to the mid-nineteenth century, the time when the Russian university and the academic intelligentsia emerged for the first time as distinctly national phenomena.

# Part Two

## THE ACADEMIC INTELLIGENTSIA AND THE PURSUIT OF *NAUKA*

This was a marvelous time — a time when everybody aspired to think, to read, and to study, and when each person of integrity desired boldly to express these feelings. Thought, previously dormant, began to awaken, stretch, and set to work. Its impulse was strong, and its tasks gigantic. There was little concern for the present; it was rather the fate of future generations, the fate of all of Russia, so dependent on future reforms, that was being discussed and resolved. This inspiring work attracted all the most gifted and independent individuals and produced a host of young publicists, writers, and scholars, the names of whom will forever be linked with the history of Russian culture and education and with the brilliant though short-lived 1860s, which for such a long time gave direction and impetus to the intellectual development of Russia.

N. V. Shelgunov[1]

The thin stratum of educated Russians responded to the "thaw" which followed the demise of Nicholas I with unprecedented enthusiasm. Youthful reformers such as the Miliutin brothers worked within the bureaucracy to prepare a series of sweeping (if incomplete) reforms of the country's basic institutions. Liberal members of "society" (*obshchestvo*) sought to carve out new areas of social activity that would be independent of bureaucratic tutelage. Students sparked the first wave of university demonstrations in Russian history and became attracted in significant numbers to radical new doctrines and bizarre patterns of personal behavior. Considerable disagreement and mistrust arose among these groups; many liberal citizens became disillusioned by the reforms actually implemented by the bureaucracy on the one hand, yet found themselves profoundly shocked by the ideas and conduct of the nihilist youth on the other. But sources of dissension should not be allowed to overshadow the large areas of agreement among forward-looking Russians during the decade of the "sixties" (as the period from 1855 to 1866 has come to be known in Russian historiography). Virtually all agreed that both reform and education were desperately needed in Russia and that indeed the two were inextricably tied together. "Russian society," stated a report signed in 1861 by several prominent Moscow professors,

> has instilled in the student a high conception of his own worth, a conception which can hardly be found in any other country. . . . At the present time every Russian person profoundly senses the need for education, as the only escape from our oppressive social ills. . . . In the eyes of many, the student represents the future hope of Russia.[2]

It was in this charged atmosphere, amidst the unleashing of long pent-up intellectual and emotional forces, that Russian science, the academic intelligentsia, and the student activist community first came of age. Among the initial acts of Alexander II which helped to revitalize the country in the wake of the Crimean debacle were measures to remove the heavy-handed restrictions which Nicholas had placed on universities as the result of 1848. Limitations on university enrollments were lifted (and in four years the size of the student body increased by almost 50 percent), courses in philosophy and European constitutional law were restored, and Russian scholars were once more permitted to study and travel abroad. The new university charter of 1863 granted professors considerably more freedom and financial support in their teaching and research. By the end of the decade, Russian scientists were making contributions of truly international significance: D. I. Mendeleev published his periodic law of chemical elements in 1869; A. M. Butlerov was contributing to the founding of modern structural chemistry; I. M. Sechenov was laying the groundwork for Pavlovian physiology; A. O. Kovalevskii and I. I. Mechnikov were engaged in pioneering work in comparative embryology.[3]

Most of these men had been trained in an earlier era, but their interests and accomplishments fitted well the positivistic intellectual atmosphere of the sixties, which exalted the natural and physical sciences as the only true source of knowledge. Nihilists such as D. I. Pisarev struck a responsive chord when they called for the extensive popularization of scientific knowledge on the grounds that rational thought was the most effective guarantor of social progress. Pisarev and other ideologists of science were instrumental in attracting scores of youths to serious university study in the sciences, thereby laying the foundation for future generations of Russian scientists.[4] One of those who began his studies at that time subsequently recalled the idealism of his fellow aspiring scientists.

If asked, "What was the most noticeable characteristic of this movement?" one can, without a moment's hesitation, answer in one word: enthusiasm. An enthusiasm that elevates and enthralls a person, a conviction that he is doing something that is capable of absorbing all of his intellectual inclinations and moral energies—something which...enters as a necessary constituent part of the much broader general movement that will guarantee the eventual elevation of the intellectual and material well-being of the public as a whole. This enthusiasm was characterized by complete selflessness, extending at times to an almost total oblivion of personal needs.[5]

The effervescent enthusiasm of the generation of the sixties proved to be short-lived. The onerous terms of the peasant emancipation of 1861, the suppression of the Polish revolt in 1863, and the attempted regicide of 1866 tended to dampen public optimism and harden official attitudes. Between the 1860s and the revolutions of 1917, public opinion in general and the social views of scientists and scholars in particular experienced broad fluctuations and significant new departures.

Yet despite the abandonment of an early and uncritical enthusiasm, despite the inroads of careerism and complacency, despite the important oscillations in emphasis from one generation to the next, the world view of Russian academics continued throughout the century to be influenced in significant ways by attitudes that originated in the sixties. The academic intelligentsia characteristically retained two basic tenets of belief: the conviction that the arbitrary and absolutist nature of autocratic power should and would be transformed through time in a more liberal direction; and a faith in *nauka* (usually understood to embrace not only science but the whole realm of scholarship in the sense of the German *Wissenschaft*) as a pursuit that would lead not only to individual intellectual rewards but also to Russian social progress and popular well being.

Thus, just as the Russian educational structure in 1917 still retained many of the features imparted to it by Peter the Great and Dmitri Tolstoi, so the outlook of the Russian academic intelligentsia continued, despite several changes, to embrace features which stemmed from the most formative stage of its development. It is to an analysis of the nature of this group, its attitudes toward *nauka* and the role of the university, and its attempts to deal with the disconcerting issue of student activism that we shall now turn.

# *3*

# THE PROFESSORIATE AND THE MYSTIQUE OF *NAUKA*

## The Russian Professoriate

The last half of the nineteenth century witnessed a steady growth in the size and significance of Russia's professional middle classes, which by the turn of the century had emerged as an articulate intellectual and political force. Professors constituted an important part of this politically liberal group, although in numbers their ranks, despite continual growth, remained relatively small. Before World War I, Russian institutions of higher education employed two to three thousand professors and privatdocents, plus an equivalent number of lower ranking teaching personnel, ranging from lecturer to laboratory assistant.[1]

Of equal importance to growth in numbers was the emergence of the Russian professoriate from its early nineteenth-century domination, so offensive to national pride, by German professors who were often ignorant of the Russian language and contemptuous of Russian conditions. The expansion of enrollments and educational facilities after the Crimean War produced an increasing stream of Russian youth anxious for an academic career. This post-Crimean generation was quick to take its place on the undermanned teaching staffs of Russian universities. By 1875 50 percent of all professors and docents were under forty years of age and 83 percent had received their first degrees from Russian universities.[2] Many young scholars continued to receive their advanced training abroad, but in the last decades before the war the government's intermittent efforts to improve university research facilities led to a substantial improvement in Russian graduate education.[3] The tendency for Russian scholars and scientists to replace foreigners is graphically illustrated by the changing composition of the Academy of Sciences, which was traditionally more foreign-dominated than the universities. During the eighteenth century only 32 percent of the academicians had been born in the Russian Empire, whereas in the nineteenth century the proportion rose to 74 percent.[4] More specifically, twenty out of twenty-three academicians elected between 1860 and 1880, and all seventy elected between 1890 and 1917, were natives of the Russian Empire.[5] Old antagonisms did not die out overnight. When the renowned chemist Mendeleev failed in 1880 to be elected to the academy by one vote, a clamor arose among the Russian scientific community which claimed Mendeleev had been defeated due to anti-Russian sentiment among foreign-born academicians. But by the end of the century the Russian academic community had achieved a self-respect which it had sorely lacked before.[6]

This newly found self-respect stemmed primarily from a growing international recognition of the many achievements of Russian science and scholarship. Despite frequent politically motivated harassment by tsarist officials and notwithstanding subsequent accusations of "senility" leveled by early Bolshevik leaders,[7] prerevolutionary Russian academic scholarship was a flourishing enterprise which contributed regularly to the international world of science and learning. It is true that some of Russia's most illustrious thinkers emigrated and did much of their important work abroad. Although I. I. Mechnikov accomplished significant research in comparative embryology during the 1860s and 1870s in Russia, he emigrated due to political difficulties in the 1880s and immediately became one of the most illustrious members of the Pasteur Institute in Paris, where he remained (winning a Nobel Prize in 1908) until his death in 1916.[8] P. G. Vinogradov, a respected authority on European medieval social history, left Moscow University for a position at Oxford. Sophia Kovalevskaia, barred by her sex from both a university education and a teaching position in Russia, was appointed full professor at the University of Stockholm and achieved European distinction as a mathematician.

Nonetheless, an impressive number of Russian scholars, while making frequent trips abroad, conducted most of their research at home, where their talents helped to raise the academic standards of Russian universities and specialized institutes to a high level. Mention has already been made of the contributions as early as the 1860s of scientists such as Mendeleev, Butlerov, and Sechenov. The most famous scientist later in the century was Ivan Pavlov, whose laboratories in the Medical-Surgical Academy attracted scientists from the West, and whose 1904 Nobel Prize for his work on digestive glands preceded his still more famous studies on conditioned reflexes. The strong Russian mathematical tradition was continued in the late nineteenth and early twentieth centuries by P. L. Chebyshev, A. A. Markov, and A. M. Liapunov. A national scientific school of soil science was formed by V. V. Dokuchaev, one of whose students, V. I. Vernadskii, became in turn one of the founders of modern geochemistry.

Nor were all the Russian contributions in the exact or natural sciences. The tsarist government did not recognize sociology as an academic discipline, but Russia boasted several internationally prominent sociologists, some of whom held precarious academic positions as professors of law. The International Institute of Sociology had in 1904 nine Russian members, five of whom had served as vice-president, and one of whom, M. M. Kovalevskii, was to serve as president in 1907. M. I. Rostovtsev became a renowned historian of the ancient Mediterranean world. Russian history was an area of intense scholarly activity, as S. F. Platonov in St. Petersburg and V. O. Kliuchevskii in Moscow stimulated scores of students to raise new questions about the Russian past. Boris Chicherin, Vladimir Soloviev, and Sergei Trubetskoi were carving out new approaches in the realm of philosophical idealism.[9]

As World War I approached, Russia was not equally strong in all disciplines. Paradoxically, the very strength of the Mendeleevan tradition in Russia inhibited the ability of Russian physicists and chemists to participate in the revolutionary new discoveries that were being made at the turn of the century. Mendeleev stubbornly regarded the new ideas concerning the divisibility and mutability of atoms as incompatible with his periodic law of the elements, and his influence prevented these ideas being pursued in Russia. It was left to a much younger generation, led by A. F. Ioffe, to assimilate the new discoveries and lay the groundwork for the subsequent achievements of Soviet physics.[10]

Although the universities were the major centers of research, their traditionalism plus the intermittent harassment by the Ministry of Public Education sometimes prevented the most talented scholars from working in them. Both Sechenov and Pavlov conducted most of their physiological research (which some governmental circles considered dangerously supportive of philosophical materialism) at the Ministry of War's Medical-Surgical Academy. Pavlov's student V. M. Bekhterev privately founded the Psychoneurological Institute, which sponsored a considerable amount of research and where M. M. Kovalevskii offered the first systematic course in sociology to be given in a Russian higher educational institution. Kovalevskii also taught at Witte's St. Petersburg Polytechnical Institute, a haven for intellectuals who could not find employment at the universities.

Although Russia was relatively weak in the applied sciences, two scholars who made great contributions in this area should be mentioned. A. N. Krylov, who taught at the Imperial Naval Academy, specialized in the structural mechanics of shipbuilding. N. E. Zhukovskii was a pioneer in developing the mathematical foundations of aerodynamics and aeronautics. The Moscow Higher Technological Academy, as the result of Zhukovskii's presence on the teaching staff, became in 1910 one of the first schools in the world to offer teaching and laboratory work in aerodynamics.[11]

While the international prestige of Russian academics was increasing, their position at home remained ambivalent. The Ministry of Education rarely let a world-wide reputation deter it from disciplinary action, as figures such as Mechnikov, M. M. Kovalevskii, and Mendeleev discovered. The 1884 university charter was another sign of the bureaucracy's distrust of its professors, since it removed most governing authority from the hands of the professors' academic councils. On the other hand, university teachers were granted privileges associated with membership in the bureaucracy. As state employees, they were enrolled on the table of ranks, which arranged all higher level military and civilian government officials on a fourteen-rung hierarchy. Their pay and prestige were improved considerably by a provision of the 1863 university charter (retained by the 1884 charter) which raised their positions two ranks (*chiny*) on the table. Thenceforth the rector of a university occupied the fourth highest rank (which automatically conferred hereditary nobility and was equivalent to the rank of major general in the military), ordinary professors occupied the fifth rank, extraordinary professors the sixth, docents the seventh, and lecturers the eighth.[12] For the practical minded, this measure provided added inducement to embark on an academic career. It may have appealed in particular to the nobility, which in the eighteenth and early nineteenth centuries had generally shunned academic pursuits on the grounds that they demanded more effort and provided fewer rewards than other forms of state service.[13] Whatever the reason, the percentage of professors of noble origin remained surprisingly constant throughout the last half of the nineteenth century, a time when the proportion of noble youth among students was declining. One study shows that at Moscow University those of noble origin constituted 65 percent of the students but only 39 percent of the professors in 1861, whereas by 1895–96 the proportion had dropped to 41 percent of students while increasing to 45 percent of professors. According to the data in another study, the percentage of teachers in all Russian universities who were noble by origin was 41 percent in 1875 and 39 percent in 1904. A much smaller proportion, however (only a quarter of all noble professors in 1875 and just 18 percent in 1904), came from the wealthier and more traditional landowning nobility.[14]

The practice of linking higher education teaching positions to both the privileges and the disciplinary power of the state bureaucracy drew sharp criticism from several different quarters. Traditional nobles had always objected to provisions in the table of ranks which permitted and encouraged the ennoblement of commoners. Student activists frequently diagnosed the reluctance of professors to support many of their demonstrations as the result of careerist instincts of *"chin*-chasing bureaucrats." Many professors themselves objected to the system on the grounds that it compromised their scholarly independence and integrity.

The fact remains, however, that neither the blandishments of bureaucratic promotion nor the preponderance of noble professors was sufficient to turn the professoriate as a whole into a completely loyal or docile group. Unlike their German counterparts, most Russian academics were either opposed in principle or at least hoped for an amelioration of the autocratic government which paid their salaries, and many viewed their pursuit of research as a means which in itself would eventually contribute to political and social reform. Of course, there were some conservative professors who actively supported the autocracy, as well as several more who simply took no interest one way or the other in broader social or political issues. Very few sympathized with student activism, much less the revolutionary parties. But a majority, including virtually all those who enjoyed the esteem and respect of their colleagues, shared a general commitment to the implementation of liberal political and intellectual values in Russia.

It is this common commitment which makes the term "academic intelligentsia," including as it does both objective occupational and subjective ideological connotations, so appropriate in describing members of this group. While rejecting radicalism, they nonetheless shared the sense of moral obligation to strive for an ideal society that was so characteristic of the entire Russian intelligentsia, broadly defined. While subscribing to the general outlook of the larger liberal intelligentsia as a whole, they, as academics, developed an additional and distinctive viewpoint of their own, which stressed the vital importance of university autonomy and the role of *nauka* in Russia's future social and cultural development. The majority of Russia's professors, in short, were more than just scholars and scientists. They formed a closely knit and articulate sociocultural group which sought to embody in its academic activities a moral commitment to progress and reform.

Indeed, the tight little world of the academic intelligentsia did not easily endure ideological defections from its ranks. When Education Minister Dmitri Tolstoi sought to revise the liberal 1863 university charter, a Moscow University physicist, N. A. Liubimov, welcomed the move, sharply criticized the existing system of university administration, and was appointed to the commission entrusted with the drafting of a new charter that would sharply restrict university autonomy. A majority of Liubimov's university colleagues thereupon sent him a collective letter announcing their decision to cut off all personal relations with him. S. A. Muromtsev, a young teacher of law who subsequently became a prominent liberal and chairman of the First State Duma, gained widespread popularity by his refusal to accept Liubimov's outstretched hand during a chance encounter at the professors' dining hall. On the other hand, another young teacher, Vladimir Soloviev, received extensive criticism for his public defense of Liubimov's right to express is opinion, whatever it may be. Soloviev, the son of the rector at that time and a subsequently famous idealist philosopher, was so stung by the disfavor of his colleagues that he resigned his position at the university.[15]

The primary vehicles for the expression of professorial views on purely educational matters were the academic councils (*uchenye sovety*), which consisted of all the tenured professors of a given higher educational institution. But members of the academic intelligentsia were also leaders of opinion on the much broader political, social, and economic issues that agitated educated society as a whole during the last half century of tsardom. Academics were frequent editors and contributors to the liberal thick journals such as *Vestnik Evropy* and *Russkaia Mysl'*. Another important outlet for professorial opinion on broad issues of the day was *Russkie Vedomosti,* a daily newspaper published in Moscow from 1864 to 1918. Taken over by a small group of progressive professors in the 1880s, it immediately became a popular rival to M. N. Katkov's conservative *Moskovskie Vedomosti,* and throughout its existence it maintained a consistent though moderate oppositionist attitude toward the autocracy.[16]

The first and only attempt to create a national organization of professors occurred during the revolution of 1905, when many professionals were defying the government by organizing national unions. An appeal to form an academic union by geochemist Vladimir Vernadskii appeared in *Russkie Vedomosti* in late 1904 and met a ready response. In January 1905, 342 St. Petersburg academics signed a declaration that strongly attacked bureaucratic interference in higher education and proclaimed that science and learning could develop in Russia only if the autocracy were transformed into a representative government. The declaration quickly circulated throughout the country, where it received nearly 1800 signatures. The first two congresses of the academic union were held in March and August of 1905, followed by a third and less successful one in January 1906. Although a large degree of agreement was achieved at the congresses, dissension developed between junior and senior faculty members, contributing to the dissolution of the union when the government recovered control after the revolution.[17]

Although professional unions did not survive the revolution, political parties did. Professors played a leading role in organizing and supporting parties having a liberal political coloration. Five professors (including Vernadskii) were among the twenty persons who attended the organizational meeting of the Union of Liberation at Schaffhausen, Switzerland, in July of 1903.[18] The twenty-six members of the first Central Committee of the Constitutional Democratic Party (hereafter known as the Kadet Party) included nine professors. Leader of the party was historian and exprofessor Paul Miliukov. Other prominent Kadets included Fedor Kokoshkin, law professor at Moscow University and editor of *Russkie Vedomosti,* Paul Gronskii, professor of law at St. Petersburg University, Vernadskii, and the historian Alexander Kizevetter, both of Moscow University. Miliukov called the Kadets a "professors' party," while Alexander Kerensky referred to it as a "faculty of politicians."[19] Several professors at the St. Petersburg Polytechnical Institute, including the well-known chemist N. A. Menshutkin and the sociologist M. M. Kovalevskii, formed a new party known as the Party of Democratic Reforms, with a program very similar to that of the Kadets.[20]

There were, to be sure, a number of conservative academics, as well as a sprinkling of socialists. Kiev University tended to be a stronghold of the right, since the autocracy had traditionally stocked its faculties with conservative Russian professors as a bulwark against Ukrainian nationalism. But political liberalism clearly predominated among the professoriate at the major university centers of Moscow, St. Petersburg, and Kazan. Well-known liberals such as Kovalevskii and Vernadskii were among those elected after 1905 to the State Council as representatives of the universities and the Academy of Sciences. The Kazan University academic council had a choice between two slates of liberal candidates to the State Council. It elected the right-leaning slate (Octobrists) in March 1906, while switching to the left-leaning slate (Kadets) in the new election of January 1907.[21] The political coloration of the academic councils can also be gauged by the way in which, after 1905, they exercised their newly regained right to elect their own rector. For example, Prince Sergei Trubetskoi, professor of philosophy, constitutional liberal, and strong advocate of university autonomy, was elected rector by the academic council of Moscow University. Upon his death shortly thereafter, he was replaced by Alexander Manuilov, professor of economics and member of the Kadet Party. Those who received this honor in other higher educational institutions also tended to be liberal in both their educational and political views.

## *Nauka* AND THE RUSSIAN ACADEMIC IDEOLOGY

The development of a Russian academic ideology during the second half of the nineteenth century was strongly influenced by academic thought and practice in Germany. The modern German university system, which developed rapidly after the founding of the University of Berlin in 1810, had by mid-century become the envy of the civilized world. France had abolished her universities during the Revolution and managed to do without them until late in the century, but both England and the United States sent their most promising young scholars to Germany for advanced training and introduced partial reforms, based on the German model, in their own long-standing university systems. The German influence was particularly strong in Russia, where universities, much later than in England or America, were taking root at the very time that the German model was enjoying its greatest prestige. Russian professors, many of whom themselves had studied in Germany, became well acquainted at an early age with the views of their German counterparts, and greatly admired the structure and functioning of the German university.

Nonetheless, there were some important differences in the typical outlooks of German and Russian academics which should be noted. The modern German university system and its accompanying academic ideology were born in the intellectual context of the upsurge of philosophical idealism of 1790–1810. Kant, Fichte, Schelling, and Wilhelm von Humboldt elaborated a concept of the proper university in which the study of philosophy, broadly understood, was to be the cornerstone. To be sure, the empirical and natural sciences became stronger than the humanistic disciplines in the second third of the century. But all disciplines, including the natural sciences, were thought to possess a moral and philosophical dimension. The main goal of education was seen to be the cultivation and cultural development of the individual, a goal which it was thought could best be achieved by illuminating the relationship between an individual discipline and the overall philosophical unity of which it was conceived to be but a part.[22]

Such sentiments were not completely absent in Russia, but the main thrust of academic thought was somewhat different. The Russian academic intelligentsia was born in the very different positivistic and even scientistic intellectual atmosphere of mid-century. Although the term *nauka* did, as a general rule, embrace humanistic scholarship, there was a tendency among some thinkers to associate it most strongly with the natural sciences. Among the leading spokesmen for higher education, one more often finds scientists than philosophers. Finally, the goal of education was more frequently expressed in terms of social progress than of individual cultivation.

One of the more extreme definitions of *nauka* was provided by the well-known biologist K. A. Timiriazev, who categorically eliminated all but the natural and exact sciences from inclusion in the term.[23] A more commonly accepted definition was written by Vladimir Soloviev, who wrote the entry on *nauka* for the authoritative Brockhaus-Efron Encyclopedia. In its broadest sense, he wrote, *nauka* is the totality of all knowledge which has been intellectually verified and systematically ordered, ranging from theology, metaphysics, and pure mathematics, to heraldry and numismatics. In its narrower sense, however, the term excludes purely factual and technical knowledge on the one hand and purely speculative constructs on the other. The proper definition of *nauka* in this narrow sense is "objectively verifiable and systematic knowledge of real phenomena (*deistvitel'nykh iavlenii*) from the point of view of their regularity or immutability (*zakonomernosti ili neizmennogo poriadka*)." Soloviev regarded the humanistic disciplines to be part of *nauka* and believed that philosophy was the sole approach capable of establishing the a priori principles and elucidating the unifying elements of all the sciences (*nauki*). But by positing verifiability, systematization, and regularity as the quintessential elements of true *nauka*, he implicitly relegated scholarship in the humanities to a secondary position.[24]

Most people both within and without the academic world did not worry about such definitional niceties, and tended to use the term *nauka* to refer generally to science and scholarship (or "learning"), as distinct from more speculative or aesthetic pursuits. That was the sense in which it was used by one author, who classified all cultural values under the four rubrics of *nauka*, philosophy, art, and ethics.[25]

Agreement was less widespread concerning the purpose, the uses, or possible benefits of *nauka* in Imperial Russia. One can discern among the educated population four basic attitudes toward the role of *nauka*. One view endeavored to disassociate the concept of *nauka* from any social or political connotations whatever. Officials in the government, constantly on the defensive from the claims of its opponents that the spirit of *nauka* was incompatible with autocracy, were the main proponents of this view. Some officials (especially in the Ministry of Finance), as well as technocratic-minded specialists, were interested in applying the fruits of *nauka* to improve the efficiency of the existing autocratic system, but their number and influence were relatively small. The tsars and their ministers of education had traditionally promoted the development of science in Russia as much to increase their European prestige as to improve their economic or military strength. Consequently, their main concern was to keep academic institutions loyal and nonpolitical. Especially after the revolution of 1905, when universities and institutes had frequently been taken over by revolutionary or highly politicized groups of students, the slogan of separating politics from *nauka* became popular with many groups on the right side of the political spectrum, including some professors.

A second view, like the first, extolled the value of pure (*chistaia*) *nauka* and disavowed any direct connection between it and political activism. But proponents of this second view, unlike adherents of the first, were tacitly opposed to the absolutism and social injustice of the existing order and believed that the pursuit of *nauka* would in and of itself lead to social progress, popular welfare, and perhaps a more liberal political system. They believed that knowledge should be widely disseminated among the population, and sometimes devoted their energy, aside from their strictly professorial duties, to this task. But primarily they were not active public or social figures, either because of personal temperament or because of the belief that *nauka* itself was both a sacred and a jealous calling that demanded one's total and undivided attention.

Thirdly were those professors who combined a similar faith in the virtues of pure science with a strong sense of social obligation to apply their specialized knowledge constantly to the problems of life. Sometimes these problems were technical; at other times they bordered on or became political. But the advocates of this view never saw their actions as benefiting narrow political or class interests. They thought that *nauka,* while standing above partisan struggles and debates, nonetheless carried within itself the seeds of a broadly liberal and democratic system, so that in working for one they were automatically benefiting the other. Their attitude was similar to that of the Kadet Party (which many of them joined), which proclaimed its *nadpartiinost'*, its determination to stand above all parties and special interests and to represent instead the interests of all the people.[26] The vast majority of the professoriate held either the second or this third attitude toward *nauka,* and virtually all of the most respected and widely known figures could be found in the third group.

Finally, there was an attitude widespread among the radical intelligentsia, though not at all among the professoriate, which proclaimed either consciously or subconsciously that *nauka* should be placed at the service of ideology and of the political struggle against tsardom. It was this view which guided most student activists and which caused much of the friction that developed between them and their mentors.

The prevailing professorial opinion concerning the relation between *nauka* and politics underwent a significant change over time. Although the predominant view contained an implicit bias in favor of political liberalism, the main political demand of the professoriate as a whole during the late nineteenth century was merely for an educational framework in which they could, by and large, govern themselves and pursue their research unhampered by ideological or political constraints. The 1863 university charter, despite some defects, granted many of these conditions. But the upsurge in student protests and the youthful revolutionary movements of the 1870s led the autocracy to think twice about the concessions to university autonomy it had made in 1863. Official commissions to revise the charter were formed as early as the mid-seventies, although their work did not bear fruit until 1884, when a new and much more restrictive charter was implemented. At about the same time a number of politically outspoken professors were removed from their positions.

The professors' academic councils frequently protested the violations of the 1863 charter that occurred before 1884 and the very nature of the new charter that went into force at that time. But until the end of the century, their collective oppositionist activity was primarily aimed at trying to persuade the autocracy to reinstate a liberal charter similar to the one of 1863.[27] Individual professors, of course, frequently expressed views and engaged in activity that was frankly antiautocratic. But it was only the combination of governmental ineptness and the rising tide of popular revolutionary sentiment in the pre-1905 era that led the professoriate as a group to proclaim that the needs of *nauka* required not just a more liberal charter but an end to the autocratic political structure itself. "It is our deep conviction that academic freedom is incompatible with the present system of government in Russia," resounded the key statement in the "Declaration of the Three Hundred Forty-two" that was signed by upwards of two thousand academics in January–February 1905. It went on to proclaim that not just partial reforms, but a radical political transformation, including an elective legislature, were necessary for academic freedom to be truly guaranteed.[28]

This position, no matter how compelling it may have been to its adherents, was not without embarrassing consequences. The professoriate, in its frequent criticisms of bureaucratic meddling, had for decades been insisting that political considerations be kept out of academic affairs. After the revolutionary tide had ebbed, right-wing publicists lost little time in attacking both liberal professors and radical students by themselves adopting a battle cry demanding the expulsion of politics from the school.[29]

The issue of the proper role of *nauka* came under intense debate at the same time by two different groups within the ranks of the intelligentsia itself. A group of prominent intellectuals, most of whom had begun as Marxists before embracing neo-Kantian and then religious views, published in 1909 a collection of essays entitled *Vekhi* (Signposts), in which they subjected to severe criticism many of the major tenets of the Russian revolutionary intelligentsia. One of the contributors, the philosopher N. A. Berdiaev, attacked the intelligentsia for its utilitarian, ideological approach to philosophy and *nauka*. Although his attack was not primarily directed against the professoriate, it nonetheless raised a number of relevant points. Rather than seeking truth as an autonomous activity which required no external justification, the intelligentsia, charged Berdiaev, subordinated this activity to a misguided effort to serve the "people," thereby unconsciously distorting or even abandoning the very search for truth itself. "Love for egalitarian justice, for the social good, for the public welfare, has paralysed love for truth [*istina*], has almost extinguished an interest in truth."[30] The typical Russian *intelligent* was interested in philosophy only to the extent that it could provide support for his already dogmatically held social views, and became enthusiastic about *nauka* only because he incorrectly believed that scientific positivism was an ideological weapon against autocracy, religion, and conservatism. In fact, argued Berdiaev, both philosophy and *nauka* demand above all the love of truth, and *nauka* itself, as created in the West, is neutral toward religion and metaphysics.[31]

The publication of *Vekhi* raised a storm of protests and a host of rebuttals from Russian *intelligenty*. One of the most relevant was written by Professor D. N. Ovsianiko-Kulikovskii, a well known cultural historian. He accepted some of the basic elements of Berdiaev's analysis, such as his distinction between perceiving a cultural phenomenon for its own sake as opposed to interpreting it as a means of satisfying one's own inner psychological or emotional needs, and his assertion that the Russian intelligentsia had traditionally approached philosophy and *nauka* from the second perspective rather than the first. Ovsianiko-Kulikovskii also agreed with Berdiaev that the first perspective was much more desirable than the second in a country having a mature culture. But he argued that in a young country, such as Russia in the nineteenth century, the second or ideological perspective toward culture is both natural and highly beneficial. In recent years, however, Russians had by and large outgrown this need, and currently the majority of the intelligentsia, he maintained, were busy accomplishing specialized tasks without recourse to the ideological frameworks of their predecessors. In a final polemical thrust, he asserted that it was precisely Berdiaev and his colleagues who were in practice attempting to revive the priority of ideology in the outlook of the intelligentsia.[32]

How are we to evaluate the positions of Berdiaev and Ovsianiko-Kulikovskii? Relatively few professors, as we have seen, actively subordinated their research to a rigidly preconceived ideological framework. Yet most of them nonetheless shared the ethos and the commitment to social progress that was characteristic of the more radical members of the intelligentsia. The professorial view of *nauka,* in fact, was a blend of the utilitarian and ideological approach which Berdiaev deplored and of the autonomous search for truth which he extolled. Ovsianiko-Kulikovskii may have been correct in his view that the ideological component in the world view of the professoriate and the intelligentsia as a whole was diminishing in recent years. Certainly the scientism of the 1860s no longer found much response among middle-aged or younger scholars by the turn of the century. Yet the fact remains that right up to 1917 most Russian professors regarded both service to the Russian people and the search for abstract truth as equally legitimate and mutually consistent motivating forces for their research. This tendency may well have influenced the approach and results of their research, and it undoubtedly distinguished them as a group from their colleagues in other countries. One Russian scientist speculated on this last point in 1916, when he wrote,

> The average German pursues *nauka* as a profitable trade — profitable not only for himself personally, but also for the people and the state. Many Englishmen and Frenchmen pursue *nauka* as an interesting and noble sport, not giving a thought to its utility. But one often finds Russians, and Slavs in general, to be motivated by a sacred enthusiasm which regards the pursuit of *nauka* as the only way to achieve a tolerable if incomplete world view, and the search for truth as both an irresistible personal need and a moral duty before the fatherland and all of mankind.[33]

Whereas commentators on the right criticized the professoriate for being overly ideological, many students harbored precisely the opposite accusation against their mentors. In 1887, demonstrating students related how they had originally arrived at the university hoping to discover knowledge which would prepare them to become fighters for the good of their native land. Instead they found *"nauka dlia nauki"* (science for science's sake) and professors who were unwilling to help them struggle against the bureaucracy.[34]

A comprehensive critique of the concept of *nauka* was contained in a collection of articles published during World War I by a group of democratic left-wing students unaffiliated with any political party. One of the major themes of the volume was the great necessity for both students and professors to engage in socially useful activity as well as study and research. The student-authors found their professors to be sadly lacking in this respect. The main reason for the existing separation they perceived between *nauka* and social activity was a widespread tendency to idolize the goddess *nauka,* a tendency, not always conscious,

> to place *nauka* beyond the limits of the commonplace, to raise it to inaccessible, sacred heights, where the noise of those "worldly agitations, passions, and battles" which becloud our vain, sinful life does not reach and, most importantly, *should not* reach. There, somewhere far away, in the blue of the sky, on a throne gilded by fantasy, clothed in the purple of the clouds, completely inundated by the rays of the sun, *she* [*nauka*] presides — eternal, impassive, imbued with divine power and beauty; while here, down below, in the dirt and semi-darkness, amidst the poisonous fumes of the earth, people swarm about, bruised by passions, dispirited by poverty and ignorance, and finding strength only in their faith in *nauka,* celebrated by them in prose and verse.[35]

The author hastened to add that he had great respect for *nauka,* but insisted that it should not be regarded as something "pure" or "superhuman," but rather as something that should be explicitly placed at the service of mankind. "Man is the measure of all things," echoed another contributor, who argued that scientific research should always be tailored to specific goals and plans rather than left to develop freely and spontaneously.[36]

The authors of this work presented a perceptive critique of that element of the professorial outlook which idolized the role of pure science. But just as critics on the right exaggerated the extent to which professors were held in thrall by ideological blinkers, these on the left overlooked the many cases where professors combined a respect for pure science with an ideologically tinged outlook that propelled them to engage in a continual round of polemical, social, and political activities. It is to a closer examination of the views and activities of five representatives of this type that we shall now turn.

# *4*

# THE ACADEMIC INTELLIGENTSIA AT WORK

### A. V. Nikitenko and N. V. Speranskii

The career of Alexander V. Nikitenko illustrates several of the paradoxes which were so abundant in nineteenth-century Russia. Born a serf, he rose to become not only professor of Russian literature at St. Petersburg University, but also an elected member of the Academy of Sciences. Friend and confidant of such literary masters as Pushkin, Turgenev, and Tiutchev, he simultaneously served the government as an official censor. Convinced that Russia's greatest need was for a great expansion of education and culture, he nonetheless maintained that the Russian people needed firm but enlightened guidance over their reading habits. He was one of a small but significant number of professors who, especially during the half-century before 1905, hoped to promote reform and enlightenment through active participation in official governmental agencies and commissions.

Nikitenko was born in a Ukrainian village in 1804, the son of an educated serf owned by the wealthy Count Sheremetev. When his family moved to Ostrogorsk, the talented son quickly drew the attention of local society, and in particular of a group of army officers, several of whom were to become leading participants in the abortive Decembrist Revolt of 1825. These individuals welcomed the young Nikitenko into their circle, and it was largely due to their efforts that in 1824 he was emancipated by his master and permitted to travel to St. Petersburg where he matriculated at the university.

It is unknown to what extent Nikitenko was aware of the developing conspiracy that led to the Decembrist uprising, for he deliberately destroyed all his diary notes for the year 1825. He must have been profoundly shocked by the tragic failure that engulfed so many of his friends and patrons. Nonetheless, through perseverance and hard work he gradually made a name for himself in the capital, and by the early 1830s had embarked on the dual careers of professor at the university and member of the censorship committee in the Ministry of Education.

There were only faint traces of political liberalism in Nikitenko's outlook. "I am a monarchist on principle (of course not an absolutist)," he wrote in 1861, in the wake of Alexander II's emancipation of the serfs.[1] He expressed his antipathy to democratic forms of government for Russia in no uncertain terms.

> I come from the ranks of the people. I am a plebeian from head to toe, but I do not entertain the thought that it is wise to give power to the people. . . . The masses will never acquire those attributes which render power just, wise, enlightened — and they will of necessity either abuse it or transfer it into the hands of one person, which would inevitably lead to despotism. The people must not rule; they must be ruled. But they must have the right to declare their needs, and to point out to the government the vices and misdeeds of those appointed to preserve and implement the laws.[2]

While committed to the principle of monarchy, however, he was unsparing in his criticism of arbitrary, arrogant, and ignorant abuses of autocratic power and unstinting in his insistence on the need for the rapid expansion of education in Russia. As early as 1828 he prepared a commentary and defense of a liberalized censorship code, a project that was aimed at achieving one of his most precious goals — "the dissemination of enlightenment and the protection of the right of Russian citizens to a free and independent inner life."[3] As a censor, he frequently opposed his more zealous and less learned colleagues, arguing that it was politically less dangerous to the regime to publish certain ideas than to prohibit them and run the risk of pushing frustrated authors closer to sedition. "Revolutions are made not by writers, but by incompetent ministers," he remarked acidly on one occasion.[4]

Nikitenko became particularly embittered at the wave of internal reaction that swept through Russia during the course of 1848. He lost his position when censorship activities were taken over by the newly created secret committee of Count D. P. Buturlin, whose zeal to stamp out all possibly disloyal thoughts led to the virtual eclipse of Russian culture during the next seven years. Wrote Nikitenko on December 2, 1848,

> Barbarism is celebrating [in Russia] its victory over the human mind, which had just begun to think, and over education, which had just begun to stand on its feet. . . . Learning [*nauka*] is becoming feeble and going into hiding. . . . A little more of this, and everything which in the course of a hundred and fifty years was accomplished by Peter and Catherine will in the end be overthrown and trampled under foot.[5]

Nikitenko was not, of course, against all censorship. What he wanted was a change from a "petty policy of threats and oppression to a policy of guidance."[6] When he was called back to government service in the 1850s, he clearly expressed his conception of what his role should be.

> In any event, I am firmly determined to fight to the end against repressive measures. But at the same time I am convinced that literature at the present moment cannot, must not cut off all connections with the government and take up an openly hostile stance against it. If I am correct, then it is necessary that one of us act to represent this connection and take on the role, so to speak, of a connecting link. I shall attempt to be this link.[7]

The extreme difficulty of this position was brought home most forcefully in 1861, when student riots led to a crisis in the relationship between St. Petersburg University, where he was a professor, and the Ministry of Education, where he was an official. He strongly opposed the student movement and was particularly disgusted by those "ultra-liberal" professors who supported it. On the other hand, he regarded the "insolence" of the students to be the natural result of the suppression of all thought during the last years of Nicholas I, and he opposed many of the punitive measures taken against them by the government and the new minister, Count E. V. Putiatin. As a member of the Bradke commission to draft a new university charter, he registered his support for full university autonomy on academic matters.[8]

Well aware of his dilemma as a moderate caught between rival camps, Nikitenko as a rule worked energetically to articulate and promote his views. His attitude is best described in his own words:

> The role of an honorable and mature person in this chaos is to stand aside from both extremes, to try to moderate now one, now the other, to observe a balance between that which blindly and irrationally tears forward, and that which drags us backward. A steadfast but reasoned liberalism, not destructive but creative — such is my motto, which emerges directly from my convictions and my character.[9]

There were times, however, when he was overtaken by self-pity, despair, and depression. "My most difficult struggle," he wrote in his diary on January 1, 1865, "is the struggle with my own *worthlessness* and, moreover, with the worthlessness of all kinds of things: social, moral, material and physical."[10] Much of his diary is pervaded by a sense of futility, combined with scathing attacks on nihilists, reactionaries, and hypocrites. His retirement from the university in 1864, after thirty years of teaching, was marked by a double-edged bitterness. Although eligible to be reelected to an additional five-year term, he declined to make such a request, convinced that his "ultraliberal" opponents within the faculty were strong enough to vote him down. The Ministry of Education thereupon made his retirement effective in June rather than September, a move which prevented him from receiving an additional 600 rubles in income. He thus felt rebuffed by both sides he had sought to serve.[11]

In some respects Nikitenko was an untypical member of the academic intelligentsia as we have defined it. His world view was formed well before the post-Crimean thaw, and as we have seen, he was frequently at odds with his more liberal colleagues at St. Petersburg University in the early 1860s. Nonetheless, he was representative of a number of professors in the last half of the nineteenth century who believed that the expansion of culture and education in Russia was more important and more feasible than liberal political reform, and who were willing to devote their considerable energies to cooperation with an autocratic government which they hoped could be persuaded to adopt and act on this commitment.

By the early twentieth century, most professors had become totally disillusioned with the tsarist government. It will be useful to examine the views of another academic who, like Nikitenko, might be termed a "cautious liberal," but who matured in this later and very different period. N. V. Speranskii, a specialist in the history of educational institutions in western Europe, wrote one of the most comprehensive theoretical statements of a liberal academic's conception of the role of *nauka* and higher education in the development of Russia. Speranskii's articles were first published in the influential "professors' newspaper," *Russkie Vedomosti,* during and after the 1911 crisis at Moscow University, in which over one hundred members of the teaching staff had resigned to protest the heavy-handed tactics of the Ministry of Education. The prevailing mood was one of intense discouragement among academics, and Speranskii sought to restate the traditional argument for autonomous universities free of governmental interference.

The shining example for Speranskii, as for most nineteenth-century scholars in Russia and elsewhere, was the German university system. Speranskii reminded his readers that the founding of the University of Berlin in the early nineteenth century was a major turning point in the development of a modern university characterized by freedom of thought and intense research devoted to important intellectual problems. He endorsed Humboldt's belief that the main purpose of the university was not so much to train specialists for the state or society as to develop in students the ability to grasp philosophically the organic unity of all branches of learning. While admitting that such a task was much more difficult in the early twentieth century than in the early nineteenth, owing to the decline of metaphysics and the growth of specialization, he nonetheless insisted that it remained a worthy goal. He considered three factors to be necessary to the fulfillment of this mission: a system of instruction which encouraged the students to work independently and creatively, rather than demanding rote memorization; freedom of the university from subordination to any external goals no matter how beneficial they may be to society and the state; and the highest degree of autonomy in all its internal affairs for the academic corporation of professors.[12]

How can one expect a government to lavish funds on an institution over which it would have so little control? Humboldt was faced with this question and argued that in the long run the state would benefit from the free development of science and scholarship. The German state governments did not always subscribe to this view, Speranskii granted, but compared to the actions of Russian ministers such as Magnitskii, Tolstoi, and Kasso, the German incursions on academic autonomy paled into insignificance. Even this friction had ended, he argued, when the government of the united empire had given its citizens the basic guarantees of a legal state and reconciled itself with its intelligentsia. Speranskii did not shrink from crediting the alliance between government and university as the basic cause for virtually all German achievements of the last fifty years—the accomplishment of political unification and the feeling of national unity, the growth of a modern economy, even Prussia's victory over university-less France in 1870.[13]

He then turned to an analysis of the Russian autocracy's contradictory attitude toward *nauka*. Although the tsars had fostered higher education during the eighteenth and nineteenth centuries, "the very spirit of *nauka*—the spirit of daring research, which does not recognize any superior authority except the laws of truth—was never congenial to the Russian government." Speranskii fondly recalled the brief period in the 1860s when the rallying cry "Freedom and Science!" (*Svoboda i nauka!*) had actually been tolerated, and when as a result, he argued, Russian learning had made great strides. Soon thereafter, however, the autocracy had returned to the hopeless task of trying to retain the benefits of *nauka* while suppressing those aspects it considered harmful. But only a truly free *nauka* can produce beneficial results, and the government's efforts had served only to arouse the bitter alienation of the intelligentsia. The situation was made still more serious by the relative lack of private capital in Russia, which made *nauka* more dependent on governmental financial assistance than in other countries.[14]

Speranskii took only small comfort in the campaign begun in 1908 to expand drastically the network of primary schools. Granting that all levels of education were important and necessary, he nonetheless insisted that the university was the single most fundamental educational institution. Primary and secondary schools were necessary to disseminate the fruits of enlightenment throughout the population, but only a university system was capable of creating and developing a national culture in the first place. The existence of such a culture was a *sine qua non* for the healthy development of both society and the state.

> Either reason [*razum*] will bring us its laws, as it has brought to other more fortunate countries, or Russia will never see bright days, or Russia will be condemned in the future to be the slaves of those peoples who recognized that there is no strength which can be compared to the strength of education, and who have converted this strength into the most important instrument in the struggle for existence.[15]

Speranskii's rosy view of the merits of the German university system has not withstood the test of time. Widespread opposition among German professors to the Weimar Republic, followed by the virtual absence of university resistance to the Nazi takeover, have prompted scholarly analyses of the nineteenth-century universities which have revised many of the views held by contemporaries.[16] It now seems clear that the German universities were not as independent of state control as it appeared at the time. One of their main functions was indeed to train professionals needed by the state, and to this end their curricula were strongly influenced by the content of the state examinations that students were required to pass before they could enter virtually any professional field. The academic corporations possessed the right only to submit recommendations for new professorial appointments, and between 1817 and 1900 nearly 25 percent of their recommendations were overruled by the state ministries.[17] Before 1914 German professors included few Jews and no Social Democrats, a situation which prompted Max Weber to remark, "In Germany the freedom of learning exists only within the limits of officially accepted political and religious views."[18]

Still, one should not exaggerate the extent to which German universities departed in practice from their ideal image. The government indeed gave them both the right and the resources to engage in pure research bearing little relevance to utilitarian ends. The superiority of their scholarly and scientific achievements in the nineteenth century remains uncontestable. It was the freedom to pursue pure research, rather than the freedom of an individual to study or profess regardless of his political or religious views, that the German professoriate extolled. For this freedom they willingly paid the price of political loyalty, incursions on their autonomy, and the teaching of professional-oriented subjects. Even in these respects, German universities were better off than those in Russia, and probably no worse than those in England or America.

More relevant for our purposes than the issue of the actual extent of the autonomy of German universities is the question of the nature of the social impact exerted by German excellence in science and scholarship. Was this academic superiority attributable to the internal organization of the universities, and was it the cause of the apparent health and strength of the German state and society toward the end of the century? Even if true, would such benefits be transferable to other countries that adopted similar educational practices? All of these propositions, which today appear highly dubious,[19] were commonly accepted at the time. To be sure, not all Russian academics shared Speranskii's enthusiasm for the political and military accomplishments of Imperial Germany or his emphasis on the need to strengthen Russian state power by means of science and education. But that the German universities were models for emulation or that the spread of *nauka* in Russia would automatically lead to social betterment were articles of faith that few thought to question.

## K. A. TIMIRIAZEV

One influential scientist who adhered to these tenets was K. A. Timiriazev, a noted plant physiologist whose political and social views placed him, unlike Nikitenko and Speranskii, on the leftward fringe of the ideology of professorial liberalism. Timiriazev's long career extended from the epoch of the great reforms to the first years of Bolshevik power, but in his outlook he always remained a man of the sixties. In 1861, as a student at St. Petersburg University, he had participated in the first student strike in Russian history, and throughout his career he remained much more sympathetic to student radicalism than did his colleagues.[20] Intellectually, he remained until his death committed to the major principles of Darwin, Marx, and Comte, three titans who dominated the intellectual life of Europe during his youth.

Timiriazev had gained international recognition for his research on photosynthesis in the late 1860s and early 1870s. But he was better known among the Russian educated public for his frequent writings which sought to popularize scientific knowledge and interpret the relationship between *nauka* and social and political issues. "From the very beginning of my intellectual activity," he wrote in 1919, "I established for myself two parallel tasks: to labor for *nauka,* and to write for the people." His commitment to educate the public on scientific matters stemmed from his belief that *nauka* and democracy would in the future go hand in hand, and that only a citizenry that was well versed in *nauka* would be able to carry out its democratic functions properly.[21]

The most concise statement of his basic beliefs can be found in the following passage.

> I profess hope, faith, and love. I love *nauka;* it alone teaches how to search for and to find the truth [*istina*]; I believe in progress—without this faith in the future, one does not have sufficient strength to endure the present. I have hope *for the young generation,* hoping that, *strengthened by knowledge,* it will lead its people along the path of progress.[22]

In their general form, these propositions were part of the intellectual outlook of virtually the entire academic intelligentsia. It will be of interest to analyze the precise connotations Timiriazev gave to them, and to note those areas in which he diverged from the views of his colleagues, as well as those in which he faithfully reflected majority opinion.

Concerning the role of *nauka,* Timiriazev to the end of his life vigorously defended doctrines which had been born in the scientistic intellectual atmosphere of the 1860s and remained for several decades important themes in the thought of the intelligentsia, but which by the turn of the century had been significantly modified by most other academic scientists. These doctrines were threefold: the belief that *nauka,* properly defined, consisted only of the natural sciences as conceived in terms of the Newtonian-mechanistic paradigm; that these sciences provided the only sound basis for knowledge in all fields; and that *nauka* thus defined was a natural ally of political democracy, which found itself opposed by reactionary political forces seeking to utilize antiscientific thought-patterns for ideological warfare.

Timiriazev thought that widespread study of the "positive sciences" was particularly important for an educated public because only they—not philosophy or metaphysics—provided the proper training for logical thought. "Only *nauka,*" he wrote, "teaches how to extract the truth from its single primary source—from reality." He extolled the English Utilitarian school, pointing out that Bentham discovered the principle of "the greatest good for the greatest number" in the thought of the eighteenth-century English chemist Joseph Priestley, and arguing that both the logic and the ethics of John Stuart Mill were based on the natural sciences.[23]

As a popularizer and defender of Darwin in Russia, Timiriazev in the 1880s encountered opponents such as N. Ia. Danilevskii and N. N. Strakhov, whose objections to Darwin's theory of natural selection were accompanied by philosophical views bearing religious and politically conservative implications. Such a combination could only have strengthened Timiriazev's conviction that science and progressive political ideas were firmly allied against a coalition of religion, reaction, and antiscientific attitudes. It was from such a relatively narrow perspective that he viewed the genetic theories and experiments of Weismann, De Vries, and Mendel. The first two of these viewed their discoveries as supplementing Darwin's theory of natural selection, and they became known as neo-Darwinists. But Timiriazev, who remained committed to Lamarckian environmentalism, initially regarded the new genetic doctrines as anti-Darwinian and even antiscientific.[24]

Timiriazev also gave a hostile reception to the new discoveries in subatomic physics and the epistemological speculation they inspired. A particularly convenient target was Sir Oliver Lodge, a prominent English physicist whose research calling into question the ether theory of light had been cited by Einstein. Lodge was elected president of the British Association for the Advancement of Science in 1913, by which time he (as well as several other prominent British physicists) had developed a strong interest in psychic research and spiritualism. In a 1914 article entitled "The Pursuit of Miracles as an Intellectual Atavism of Men of Science," Timiriazev scathingly criticized Lodge for his willingness to consider the possible existence of nonscientific ways of approaching the truth.[25]

Timiriazev, of course, was only one of many respected scientists throughout the world who rejected the initial discoveries in the fields of genetics and subatomic physics. He went much further than most, however, when he encrusted his scientific views with simplistic political dogmas. In 1919 he attacked once again such "degenerative" intellectual currents of the recent past as "the pursuit of miracles (Lodge), the backward movement from reason to instinct (the intuition of Bergson), the return to vitalism and glorification of Mendelism in biology." "For the attentive observer," he continued,

> these signs of regression in scientific thought, together with the similar movement in the area of art and literature, were only a particular manifestation of the long-premeditated clerical-

capitalistic and political reaction. All the forces of darkness united against two forces, to which the future belongs: in the area of thought, against *nauka;* in life, against socialism.[26]

Although the intensity of these views may have been influenced by the catastrophe of World War I, the dispute with his liberal colleagues which occurred at this time (discussed below), and the Bolshevik Revolution, they nonetheless represent a logical extension of his earlier outlook.[27]

More widely shared by the Russian academic community at this time was Timiriazev's characteristically liberal faith in human progress and his belief that it would be strongly abetted by the spread of both knowledge and democracy. In an article published in 1907 he wrote that the Darwinian "struggle for existence" among animals does *not* necessarily extend to humans, who have the capability of substituting elections and intellectual persuasion for such a struggle. The word, when it is based on true enlightenment, can be stronger than the deed. Universal suffrage plus freedom of speech provide guarantees, he argued, that sooner or later reason will prevail and progress occur.[28]

Timiriazev admired the development of civil and political liberties in the West, and the university systems of England and Germany. He placed a high value on academic freedom, but believed that it could exist only in a country where true civil liberties were guaranteed. Citing N. I. Pirogov's dictum that universities, as barometers of society, were able to reflect but not alter existing social and political forces, Timiriazev arrived, sooner and more forcefully than many others, at the conclusion contained in the appeal of the professors' academic union in early 1905: that only a transformation of the autocratic government, not just a new university charter, could guarantee the necessary environment for education and *nauka*. He drew the implication from this conclusion with characteristic bluntness: a scholar must become involved with politics because education is one part of which politics is the whole.[29]

Timiriazev viewed university self-government as a necessary component of academic freedom, but his interpretation of the concept of autonomy differed in one significant aspect from that of the majority of his liberal colleagues. Stressing that the right of professors to elect their own members was one of the most "responsible" and "sacred" of their duties, he continued,

> Only under conditions of complete control by social opinion, only when the election process is completely open and public ...only when all these guarantees are observed will the very

important process of professorial self-government serve to guarantee a high intellectual and moral stature in the representatives of university *nauka*.

By placing the autonomy of university professors at the behest of "social opinion," Timiriazev echoed the earlier concerns of Pirogov that academic councils if isolated from the public would drift into nepotism and stagnation and foreshadowed his own subsequent support for early Bolshevik university policies.[30]

Yet while insisting that the goal of *nauka* is to serve the people, that the scholar must get involved in politics, and that society must exercise some control over the autonomy of universities, Timiriazev wholeheartedly supported the position that the scientist should be completely free to pursue his research, unhampered by political constraints or utilitarian demands. Pure science follows its own inner logic of development, he argued, and can progress only when given complete freedom. Scientific discoveries do not result from the pressure of economic needs or the demands of technology, but rather the reverse is true — the main advances in applied sciences invariably stem from breakthroughs at the theoretical level.[31]

Timiriazev's attitude on these questions highlights an apparent paradox in the outlook of the entire academic intelligentsia. On the one hand, they defended the free pursuit of pure science, while on the other hand they professed their major commitment to be service to the people (*narod*). The seeming inconsistency is explained by their belief that it was precisely pure science that would ultimately bring the greatest popular benefit. Although with hindsight one might question the correctness of this conviction in the Russian context, it was defended at the time by two major arguments. First, Timiriazev and most Russian scholars thought that the study of pure science involved the cultivation in the student of a critical scientific attitude in general, which would lead to a questioning and eventual rejection of the autocracy and the values on which it was based. They sought to cultivate such an attitude not only among their university students, but also among the educated public as a whole by the public dissemination of research results either through the press (Timiriazev's primary medium) or through voluntary participation in public lecture series, women's higher courses, or "people's universities." This attitude contrasted sharply with that of the German professoriate, which traditionally had tended to emphasize the esoteric and impractical aspects of pure science as a means of shielding their activity from public gaze and of preserving a sacred image of their activity.[32]

Secondly, Russian academics gave the highest priority and prestige to pure science precisely because, as already indicated, they thought the major advances in the practical applications of knowledge were the result of initial breakthroughs at the theoretical level. They were not opposed to applied science as such, and indeed, the number of professors who eagerly sought to apply their knowledge in socially useful ways is impressive. Of the members of the juridical faculty of Moscow University in the late 1870s, for example, A. I. Chuprov played an active role in creating the field of zemstvo statistics, I. I. Ianzhul helped draft Russian factory legislation and actually became a factory inspector in the 1880s, while S. A. Muromtsev, despite having the relatively arcane specialty of Roman law, devoted himself to furthering the development of legal consciousness in Russia by establishing a broadly based legal society with its own journal.[33] Many natural scientists shared the same type of commitment. In particular, Dokuchaev's school of soil science had many practical applications, and his students V. I. Vernadskii and F. Iu. Levinson-Lessing became champions of applied as well as theoretical research. If on the whole Russian applied science, and in particular the relationship between industry and physics or chemistry, was extremely weak, the fault lies not so much with the scientists, some of whom criticized the situation, as with the government, which could not be persuaded to provide the needed funding. Peter the Great had founded the Academy of Sciences partially in the belief that it would provide valuable scientific advice to the government. Yet over the course of two hundred years the autocracy rarely was interested enough to ask its advice. The situation became critical during World War I, when Russia's previous dependence on German technology became clearly evident. It was on the initiative not of the government but of Vernadskii, who had become an academician in 1909, that the Academy of Sciences in 1915 established the Commission for the Study of Natural Productive Forces (KEPS), which worked out emergency plans for scientific assistance to war industries and prepared to undertake a systematic survey of Russia's productive resources.[34] The major inconsistency, therefore, appears to be not just the professoriate's combined pursuit of pure research and service to the people, but also the autocracy's willingness to fund pure research while being relatively indifferent to its possible military or industrial applications.

The government's support even for pure research was, of course, shaky at best. The 1911 crisis at Moscow University set off a flurry of demands by those who had resigned, including Timiriazev, Vernadskii, and P. N. Lebedev, for the establishment of private research institutes that would free scientists both from the arbitrary whims of the bureaucracy and from the time-consuming burdens of university teaching. Citing the existence of such institutes in Germany, England, and America, Timiriazev was particularly concerned that Lebedev, Russia's leading physicist at the time, should have a laboratory in Moscow that would enable him to continue his research. In response to this need, influential scientists and private donors founded in 1911 the Moscow Society for a Scientific Institute, an organization dedicated to the establishment of a network of privately supported research facilities.[35]

The subsequent development of the enterprise, however, took a fateful turn which led to the alienation of Timiriazev, his severing of relations with many of his former associates, and a further sharp push to the left in his political ideology. Lebedev died in 1912, and the leadership of the task of planning a new physics institute under the auspices of the Moscow Society for a Scientific Institute was assumed by one of his students, P. P. Lazarev. When the laboratories of the Physics Institute opened in January 1917, Timiriazev and several other scientists found themselves denied access to the facilities. A long-time contributor to *Russkie Vedomosti,* Timiriazev immediately wrote an article to protest the policy of the institute, only to have the newspaper refuse to publish it. The editor was the economist A. A. Manuilov, a prominent liberal who in 1911 had been removed from his position as rector of Moscow University by Education Minister Kasso, thereby sparking the mass resignations of that year, and who subsequently was to become (as a Kadet) himself Minister of Education under the Provisional Government. Manuilov had been closely involved in the establishment of the Moscow Society for a Scientific Institute, and completely supported Lazarev's policies. Timiriazev reacted with righteous indignation because he had envisaged the institute as an "asylum for free science," open to all, and would have been assured an honored place in it had his friend Lebedev lived. He quickly branded Lazarev a "monopolist" and regarded the support of his actions by the liberal editors of *Russkie Vedomosti* as one of the most "shameful" acts in the history of education. Whereas the destruction of Moscow University in 1911, he wrote, illustrated the fate of *nauka* when left to the mercy of tsarist bureaucrats, Lazarev's dictatorship over the Physics Institute demonstrated that *nauka* was no freer when controlled by private capitalists.[36] Such a conclusion helped to determine Timiriazev's negative attitude toward the Provisional Government and his subsequent support of Bolshevik rule.

## V. I. Vernadskii and A. A. Kizevetter

More typical of liberal professors during the period before the Revolution were the geochemist Vladimir I. Vernadskii and the historian Alexander A. Kizevetter. Both having attended university during the 1880s, they were of a younger generation than Timiriazev, and were at the peak of their careers and influence in 1905–17. They both were members of the Central Committee of the Kadet Party during this period, their political activism thereby being similar in orientation though more extensive in practice than that of their colleagues. Kizevetter was elected a deputy to the Second Duma, whereas the academically more eminent Vernadskii was elected to the State Council as a representative of the Academy of Sciences and higher educational institutions. Vernadskii became an assistant minister of education under the Provisional Government, while Kizevetter influenced public opinion as a sometime editor and frequent contributor to the journal *Russkaia Mysl'* and the newspaper *Russkie Vedomosti*. Both opposed the Bolshevik takeover, but whereas Vernadskii renounced politics and remained in the Soviet Union (where he died in 1945), Kizevetter, after experiencing considerable political harassment, emigrated to Prague in 1922.

Vladimir Vernadskii was one of a line of distinguished scholars. His father, a political economist of Ukrainian origin, taught at Kiev and Moscow universities and the St. Petersburg Technological Institute, whereas his son George emigrated after the Revolution to become, at Yale University, one of the outstanding historians of Russia in the Western world. Vladimir himself, in view of his pioneering studies in geochemistry, was elected an adjunct to the Russian Academy of Sciences in 1906 and a full academician in 1909. Many of his experiences were typical for a member of the Russian intelligentsia of his generation. As a student at St. Petersburg University in the early 1880s, he helped found a small circle (*kruzhok*) of comrades who were united by a common intellectual outlook and intense emotional ties. Vernadskii's liberal and scholarly inclinations were already evident in the program of the circle. Known as the *Bratstvo "Priiutino"* ("The Brotherhood of Shelter"), it devoted itself to the dual goals of the pursuit of modern science and learning plus the achievement of political reforms through nonterroristic means. Graduation from the university did not put an end to the circle, whose members continued until 1917 to assemble annually for a traditional gathering the night before New Year's Eve. There was considerable intermarriage among families of the members, but perhaps the most salient evidence of the group's homogeneity of outlook was its contribution to the leadership ranks of both the Kadet Party and the academic world. Of the group's original nine or ten members, four were subsequently elected to the Kadet Central

Committee: Vernadskii, S. F. Oldenburg, A. A. Kornilov, and Prince D. I. Shakhovskoi. Oldenburg was an orientalist who became Secretary of the Academy of Sciences and Kerensky's Minister of Education (it was he who invited Vernadskii to serve as assistant minister), whereas Kornilov and I. M. Graves (Grevs) were historians. In addition to their political and academic work, most *"Priiutintsy"* were active in disseminating knowledge to the public. They worked on behalf of the spread of primary and secondary education throughout the empire, and Vernadskii, Graves, and Oldenburg all were active in sponsoring or teaching women's higher courses.[37]

As a scientist, Vernadskii welcomed the revolutionary developments of 1890–1910 and the epistemological limitations they seemed to place on the positivistic outlook. But while admitting that *nauka* was not the only possible source of truth or cultural values, he nonetheless placed great emphasis on the growth and dissemination of scientific and technical knowledge as a development which he thought would go hand in hand with democracy in ensuring social progress.[38] Indeed, he thought that "the first and most basic task of higher education is the rapid and complete communication of the discoveries of *nauka* [and by *'nauka'* he usually meant 'science' narrowly defined] and technology to the broadest possible layers of the young and adult population, the inculcation of this knowledge into their consciousness so that the results of this knowledge can be rapidly put to use in life."[39] Vernadskii observed that over the past fifty years the Western world had experienced a growing democratization, by which he meant both the emergence of democratic governments and an increased respect for individuality. While not denying that religious or philosophical traditions had an influence on this democratization process, he nonetheless argued that it was a primary consequence of "scientific successes and the growth of scientific knowledge and scientific technology." "In its very basis," he continued,

> *nauka* is profoundly democratic, because it has as its source only the mental ability and inspiration of an individual person, and its results are absolutely not connected with any particular kind of social system. For *nauka* the most beneficial and desirable social systems are those which make possible, on the one hand, the freest scope for highly gifted personalities, and on the other, permit the fullest realization of the organization of collective scientific work, utilizing for this the life of every human individual.[40]

If *nauka* and higher education were instruments of democratization, how then did Vernadskii analyze their role in autocratic Russia? There

89

was a real contradiction, he wrote in 1913, between the profoundly nondemocratic framework of Russian life and the true nature and needs of *nauka* and the university. This contradiction had produced the current crisis in higher education. But Vernadskii had no doubt that in the long run the contradiction would be resolved by *nauka*'s achieving the transformation of the autocracy, rather than vice versa.[41] He saw the power of *nauka* in modern society as pervasive and ever-growing. "The organization of scientific work and the system of higher education will everywhere with each passing year become increasingly powerful factors in universal culture, increasingly penetrating modern society and inculcating themselves into social and governmental life."[42] Even while chronicling the Russian government's repressive policies against higher education during the years 1911–13, he sought to give heart to his readers by stressing the simultaneous creative activity of the liberal public in establishing and staffing new educational and research institutions. The continuation of this fruitful activity despite all the obstacles erected by the government, he argued, gave ample grounds for optimism that the creative forces of the people would in the end prove victorious over the repressive actions of the autocracy.[43]

Vernadskii ardently supported the widest possible spread of education. He envisioned the *"sozdanie uchashchagosiia naroda"*—the active involvement of the entire Russian people in educational pursuits. Although he did not specify the particulars of how such an objective could be achieved, he did call for the encouragement and further expansion of "people's universities" and other public-sponsored activities designed to provide adult education at all levels.[44]

The great emphasis which he placed on the large-scale dissemination and the practical application of knowledge in no way lessened the importance he attached to pure research and traditional university education. He regarded universities, devoted as they were to both research and teaching in broad areas of human knowledge, as playing the most central role in higher education. While granting that the relatively new polytechnic institutes possessed many positive features, he argued that neither they nor the more specialized technical institutes should be allowed to dominate the higher educational system. Universities had proven their worth in Europe and North America and were no less vital to Russia. He saw their importance as twofold: they alone provided a general rather than a specialized education at the highest level; and they alone promoted within society at large a respect for pure knowledge.[45]

In 1884 a young and impressionable Alexander Kizevetter journeyed from the remote provincial town of Orenburg to enter the historical-philological faculty of Moscow University. Already having decided to become a scholar in Russian history, he was irresistibly drawn to Moscow by the name of V. O. Kliuchevskii as well as by the university's past association with such great figures in Russian culture as T. N. Granovskii, Alexander Herzen, Sergei Soloviev, and Constantine Aksakov. Subsequently recalling his feelings at the time, Kizevetter wrote, "I entered the university with a genuinely religious feeling, as though entering a temple, full of sacred treasures."[46]

Like Vernadskii, Kizevetter early displayed a devotion to *nauka* and to liberal political views, combined with a disinclination to participate in the desultory student or revolutionary movements of the 1880s. This was a period when a majority of intelligentsia youth rejected the revolutionary path of the seventies, concentrating instead on "small deeds," described by Kizevetter as the patient, slow, molecular work of constructing new social forms and social relations. This type of activity did not at all signify a renunciation of the intelligentsia's traditional "civil obligation" (*grazhdanskaia povinnost'*), argues Kizevetter, who clearly felt such an obligation throughout his career. Rather, it reflected the conviction that engagement in "small deeds" was the only way to achieve *any* results under the present circumstances. By the decade of the nineties, therefore, a whole generation was ready to take advantage of those forms of legal social activity that were becoming possible.[47]

One example of the "small deeds" in which Kizevetter and many of his colleagues became involved during the 1890s was the creation of a university extension system for Russia. Impressed by the existence of extension courses in the United States and England, the historian Paul Miliukov, assisted by the volunteer efforts of other eminent Moscow scholars such as the biologist M. A. Menzbir and the historian P. G. Vinogradov, undertook to establish correspondence courses that would cover the regular four-year university course in all subjects except medicine. Kizevetter, then teaching part time at secondary level institutions while finishing his master's dissertation, took an active role with other young scholars from various disciplines in compiling syllabi and textbooks for the courses. When a lecture bureau was established, he took his turn in giving lecture series on academic subjects in the provinces and subsequently became chairman of the bureau. One can well imagine that work of this kind, as Kizevetter subsequently recalled, played a strong unifying role in the intellectual and social formation of his generation of university scholars.[48]

Although repeatedly harassed by central and local officials, the Commission for the Organization of Home Study (as, with purposeful innocuousness, it was titled by its founders) met with a ready response from the educated public. The founders were determined not to simplify or in any way water down the high university level of the studies, so subscribers primarily consisted either of those who had completed secondary but not higher education, or those who had attended a higher educational institution but were interested in a different specialty from the one they had studied. The correspondence courses and traveling lecturers were undoubtedly a particular boon to those of curious intellect who found themselves in isolated provincial backwaters.[49]

The commitment of those who staffed the courses and the eagerness of those who subscribed to them are thus beyond doubt. Yet one might still question, as some did at the time, the propensity of the academic intelligentsia to devote more of their extracurricular efforts to the spread of new forms of higher education such as extension courses or women's higher courses than to the expansion of the primary or secondary educational sector. Some reasons for this tendency are fairly self-evident. It was obviously easier and more natural for a professor to do his extra teaching at a university level rather than on a lower plane. It is also true that the government reacted more negatively to academic efforts to promote mass education than it did to the extension concept. After all, the Sunday-school movement of the early sixties and the literacy committees of the nineties both bore the brunt of considerable bureaucratic hostility.[50]

But there was still another reason, more closely connected with the professors' ideology, for their strong attachment to educational expansion at the higher level. N. V. Speranskii's view that a large university system was essential to the development of a national culture has already been mentioned. Kizevetter argued in much the same vein:

> But we [the professors organizing the extension courses] could not possibly agree with the rather wide-spread opinion that higher education was a kind of luxury, a kind of intellectual gourmet dish, that the country could do without until more essential tasks were accomplished. No one can deny the necessity for the broadest possible dissemination among the masses of primary and secondary education. But just as urgent a necessity is the attraction of the greatest number of people to higher education, for only in that event does a genuine increase of culture occur in the given country.[51]

Yet in virtually all spheres of high-level "culture," Russians at this time were making European-wide contributions. Figures presented in chapter 2 demonstrate that Russia had the highest ratio of university students to primary pupils of any major European country at that time. Primarily due to the nongovernmental efforts of private citizens, the overemphasis on higher as opposed to primary education continued to increase during the last two decades before the Revolution. Academics and other liberal *intelligenty* may have genuinely felt a commitment to the masses, but in practical terms their educational activities primarily benefited educated society.

Perhaps a more significant example of this type of activity was the establishment of Shaniavskii University in 1908 by private and public initiative. A. L. Shaniavskii was a wealthy retired general who dreamed of establishing a private higher educational institution that would be free of bureaucratic tutelage. Influential liberal professors such as A. I. Chuprov, M. M. Kovalevskii, S. A. Muromtsev, A. A. Manuilov, and N. V. Speranskii helped to plan and organize the institution. Although the Minister of Education, A. N. Schwartz, succeeded in restricting some of the institution's hoped-for autonomy, it nonetheless was able to introduce a number of interesting innovations in educational practice. First and foremost was its admissions policy. The only requirement was that students be at least sixteen years of age. They could be of either sex, any nationality or religion, and need not have graduated from a secondary school.[52] Prospective students were simply warned that courses were taught on a university level and that therefore a secondary-school level of preparation was presumed. If a student without such preparation nevertheless wanted to enroll and attend classes, he was welcome. Examinations were not compulsory, and the completion of the university course and examinations did not entitle a student to any rights other than a certificate attesting to this accomplishment. Kizevetter relates, however, that a Shaniavskii certificate was highly regarded by many employers. He further states that the university was used as a recruiting center by officials from distant provinces, who were intent upon hiring students, even before they had completed their course of study, to staff their provincial libraries and cooperatives.[53]

The finances of the university came partly from Shaniavskii's endowment, partly from public and private donations, and partly from tuition payments. The size of the tuition was set by the university council, and could be waived in the event of sufficient funds from other resources.[54]

The Shaniavskii experiment provides a convenient touchstone by which one can gauge the attitudes of Kizevetter and his closest colleagues toward the concept of *nauka* and the role of higher education. An enthusiastic supporter of Shaniavskii (Kizevetter's lectures there on Russian history drew up to one thousand listeners), he nevertheless viewed that kind of institution as only a supplement, not a substitute, for the regular network of state universities. In the opinion of the founders of Shaniavskii, the two types of institutions should have fundamentally different aims. State universities, they believed, had two main tasks. One was to serve the needs of the state apparatus by providing trained jurists, teachers, doctors, and bureaucrats. (Not all liberal professors, however, agreed that this was a proper task of state universities.) The second task, of course, was the promotion of *nauka,* and "*nauka* has special requirements which are a necessary condition for its flourishing and development, but which do not have any close, direct connection with the interests of the broad, social masses."[55]

The tasks of the Shaniavskii University, on the other hand, were to disseminate a knowledge of *nauka* among the people as a whole and to develop new knowledge in those areas where it could help provide solutions to current social problems. An example of the latter task was the scholarly study of the cooperative movement, which was one of the specialties of Shaniavskii University. The two types of higher educational institutions, Kizevetter maintained, were therefore complementary and should exist side by side.[56]

Kizevetter thus supported pure research in the state universities even when it gave no immediate promise of having practical applications. His choice of a field for his own research, however, reveals that he was influenced by contemporary political concerns. The general topic for both his master's and doctoral projects was the development of local self-government in eighteenth-century Russia, a theme which required years of extensive archival research. He explained his choice of this topic by his conviction that sooner or later the Russian autocracy would be transformed into a constitutional government, and it therefore behooved the historian to search for historical precedents in Russia's past. Although neither Muscovy nor the Russian Empire had had constitutional forms in its central governmental structure, they both had allowed a certain amount of local self-government. Furthermore, city self-government in the Medieval West had turned out to be a prototype of constitutional government—a development which he obviously hoped would occur, helped perhaps in some small way by his own research, in Russia.[57]

# 5

# CONFRONTING STUDENT
# ACTIVISM

THE SAME FACTORS WHICH CONTRIBUTED TO THE FORMATION OF A UNIQUE mentality among Russia's professors—an erratically oppressive autocratic system, an elitist educational network based on Western models, the ever-present allure of Western ideas—also helped to shape a distinctive outlook on the part of Russia's student youth. In some important respects, however, the *Weltanschauung* of student activism differed from that of professorial liberalism. Students had great respect for knowledge but were not always satisfied with what they received from the lecture podium and were not as convinced as their mentors that pure learning (*chistaia nauka*) would in and of itself lead directly to the public good. Impatient in their determination to bring about rapid change, student activists more frequently viewed the university as a staging ground for protest than as an autonomous temple of learning.

The distinctive mental outlook and group solidarity of the student body first coalesced in the post-Crimean atmosphere and soon began to manifest itself in mass demonstrations. The first of these occurred at St. Petersburg University in 1861, and for the next fifty years student mass meetings, protest marches, strikes, conflicts with police, arrests, and expulsions kept Russian higher education in a state of nearly constant turmoil. Although activists did not always constitute an absolute majority of the student population, they generally were able to dominate the student body and create a cult of self-sacrifice which assured that replacements would always be found for those who were constantly being expelled or arrested. A brief overview will give some idea of the scope of movement. In 1861 some 300 St. Petersburg students were arrested, 659 suspended, and the university was closed for two years.[1] Widespread disturbances erupted again at various higher educational institutions in 1869, 1874, and 1879. The first half of the eighties was relatively quiet, but 1887 witnessed a new series of demonstrations, and in 1890 over 500 students were arrested in St. Petersburg alone.[2] Nine years later a widespread student strike initiated a new period of turbulence that reached crisis proportions. Close to 25,000 students from thirty institutions took part in the strike of 1899, many of them suffering arrest, exile, or expulsion.[3] Students participated freely in the events of the 1905 revolution, when university halls served briefly as founts for revoutionary oratory. The last major protest occurred in 1910-11, having been sparked by clashes with authorities during a large student march at the funeral of Leo Tolstoi.

The student movement placed liberal professors in a most uncomfortable dilemma. To the extent that it was directed against the arbitrary actions of the autocracy or its Ministry of Education, it could receive the sympathy if not active support of the faculty. But to the extent that it interfered with normal educational activities, asserted the right to make basic educational policy decisions on its own, or utilized educational facilities for explicitly political goals, it conflicted with dearly held professorial convictions. Caught in the middle between students and the autocracy, frequently condemned by both sides, professors found their goal of an autonomous, faculty controlled university to be frustratingly elusive.

## THE STUDENT MOVEMENT, 1855-1914

Although basic political issues were never far beneath the surface, most of the demonstrations before the turn of the century were ignited by conflicts on purely educational matters. The two most important bones of contention were the autocracy's reluctance to permit students to form autonomous organizations, and its intermittent efforts to discourage indigent students by increasing the costs of higher education.

The 1835 university charter had strictly forbidden any student meeting or cooperative activity outside of the classroom. In the post-Crimean atmosphere, however, this restriction was widely ignored by students and indulgently overlooked by administrators and professors. As a result, a host of student organizations and activities sprang up in the late fifties. The first to appear were those which ministered to student financial and daily needs, such as loan banks and cafeterias. Soon student collective action began to move into more sensitive areas. Conflicts with the police occurred, and students as a group began to boycott professors whom they deemed either incompetent or politically unacceptable. *Skhodki*, mass student meetings with no formal rules of procedure where students voted on collective action, were held more and more frequently. When an alarmed government responded in May 1861 with a host of ordinances which reiterated the ban on unauthorized meetings and drastically reduced the size of the state scholarship system, the lines were drawn for the massive confrontation at St. Petersburg University that followed.[4]

The extent of student activism alarmed not only the autocracy, but also the majority of the professoriate. The new university charter of 1863, which granted extensive rights of self-administration to professors, left the formulation and administration of student disciplinary rules to organs which were elected by the faculty of each university. A ministerial directive made it clear that highly restrictive regulations were expected, and the university academic councils proved more than willing to oblige by passing nearly identical sets of regulations which severely restricted students' rights to form autonomous organizations.[5]

Students were not inclined to relinquish easily the rights to collective action which they had enjoyed however briefly before 1861. Fairly typical was the pattern of conflict which repeated itself at the St. Petersburg Technological Institute in 1861-62, 1868-69, and 1874. A group of students would hold an illegal *skhodka* to protest their lack of rights. The administration of the institute would suspend or expel the leaders of the *skhodka,* whereupon this disciplinary action would prompt sympathy demonstrations by a much larger contingent of the student body.[6] Frequently demonstrations in one higher educational institution would spread to others. When students at the Kharkov Veterinary Institute were arrested in 1878 while protesting the arbitrary actions of one of their professors, their cause was quickly taken up by students throughout the entire country.[7]

In view of the continuing outbreak of demonstrations in the sixties and seventies, Dmitri Tolstoi and other autocratic officials concluded that the professors and university administrators were being too lax in their enforcement of disciplinary rules. Consequently, the 1884 university charter placed disciplinary responsibility in the hands of a small board of university officials who were appointed by the ministry rather than elected by the faculty. The principle of no corporate rights for students was strongly reaffirmed.[8]

Regardless of the principle, however, it proved impossible effectively to prohibit students, most of whom had come from all parts of the country and had found themselves strangers and alone in the city, from congregating in groups of various types. Aside from the ephemeral *skhodki,* a number of student associations continued to exist. The most innocuous (except when they were consciously taken over by radical students) were the barely tolerated mutual aid societies — the student-run banks, libraries, dormitories, and cafeterias. The most dangerous, from the point of view of the regime, were the so-called circles of self-education.

It was in the underground circles of self-education that the two communities of student activists and nonstudent revolutionaries overlapped. During the 1860s most student activists had rejected the demands of a minority that student protest be diverted into explicitly political and revolutionary channels. Nonetheless, the broad student movement proved a fertile training and recruiting ground for the narrower ranks of those committed to radical dissent. Radicals shared the prevailing belief of the sixties that knowledge was a prerequisite to meaningful social change, but they were dissatisfied with the knowledge dispensed in university lectures by professors whom they regarded as tools of the bureaucracy. Instead, they organized informal study circles in which the curriculum consisted primarily of forbidden works by Western and Russian social thinkers. Many participants eventually dropped out of formal educational institutions in order to devote their lives to the revolutionary cause. Though loosely organized, a national network of study circles had developed by the seventies which exchanged ideas, disseminated illegal publications, and helped to mobilize participants in the "to the people" campaigns. Similar circles continued to be important for several decades in establishing the social and intellectual context for radical dissent among the youth of Russia.[9]

More typical and important for the strictly student population were the so-called regional circles (*zemliachestva*), which consisted of students who hailed from a common hometown or region. These groups first arose in the 1860s and grew rapidly during the rest of the century. During the 1890s they began to guide and direct a new upsurge in student unrest. In 1892 Moscow University had 43 regional circles with a total membership of some 1700 students. Each circle elected a representative to a united council (*soiuznyi sovet*), which often acted as a spokesman for students. The council attempted to adjudicate disputes between students and professors and did not hesitate to ostracize certain professors for having reactionary political views. Nonetheless, the outlook of the council proved more cautious than that of most of the regional circles and only in 1896 did it reluctantly begin to provide organizational support for student demonstrations.[10]

A nation-wide student strike erupted in February of 1899 after a group of St. Petersburg University students were beaten by police while demonstrating in support of student rights. The strike was suppressed, but although calm briefly returned during the academic year 1899–1900, the following years witnessed renewed conflict between students and government. Minor concessions to student rights granted by the autocracy in 1899, 1901, and 1902 were more than offset by the widely detested action in 1901 of temporarily drafting into the army some 200 students who had been expelled for participation in disorders. By 1903 and 1904 the traditional student organs in many universities were led by representatives of the illegal political parties that were emerging in the country as a whole at that time: Socialist Revolutionaries, Social-Democrats, Liberals (*Osvobozhdentsy*).[11]

Not all students were attracted to such parties. There remained a significant number of student activists, now known as academicists (*akademisty*), who opposed the adoption of political and revolutionary goals by the student movement. Similar to those advocates of economism who urged the labor movement to give priority to economic rather than political demands, student-academicists argued that students should concentrate their efforts on educational issues such as student rights and revision of the 1884 university charter. Finally, there were some students who were either opposed or indifferent to the entire student movement regardless of whether it was academic or political in nature. Efforts by activists to enforce student strikes by obstructing university entrances or interfering with lectures elicited conflict with nonstriking students, opposition from professors, and the frequent intervention of police.[12]

It was the politically oriented students, however, who gained the most momentum during the fast-moving events of 1904–5. Bloody Sunday (January 9, 1905) constituted the final straw that induced the vast majority of students throughout the country to strike in the pursuit of political goals. A mass *skhodka* at St Petersburg University on February 7, overruling the objections of a few dozen supporters of "pure learning," called for the formation of a constituent assembly and resolved to curtail classes until the fall of 1905 to enable students to devote themselves to revolutionary activities in their home districts. Most professors and university administrators now became convinced that a return to normal academic activities was impossible and refused to cooperate with governmental efforts to force a resumption of classes in February. Rumors began to circulate that the government intended to retaliate by firing all professors and expelling all students. Instead, an April conference of ministers and State Council members adopted a less drastic course: all students would be permitted to resume their studies in the fall and would not be charged tuition for the cancelled spring semester, but additional interruptions of classes in the fall would be met with mass expulsions of students and dismissals of professors.[13]

But the tumultuous events of fall, 1905, led to situations which few could have predicted. Institutions of higher education became directly involved in the thick of revolutionary activity for the first and only time in their history, and there occurred a sharp reversal of attitudes by students and authorities on the question of whether they should remain open or be closed. The single most important cause was the rising tide of revolutionary fever, which broke into a general strike in early October and forced the issuance of the imperial manifesto of October 17, wherein the tsar promised to introduce the trappings of constitutional monarchy. Concerning higher education, there were two decisive events — the government's granting of university autonomy on August 27, and the decision the following month by students throughout Russia to replace demands for a student strike and continued closure of universities with demands that the universities be "opened up" and utilized for revolutionary activity as well as normal classes.

The government's concession of university autonomy not only granted the professors' academic councils the right to elect their own rector and deans, but also returned to them exclusive control over student disciplinary action. This meant that the police would be no longer able legally to enter university premises unless specifically invited by elected university officials. Higher educational institutions thereby acquired a certain immunity that was unique in all of Russia. Social-Democrats appear to have been the first to see the possibilities inherent in the new situation. Traditionally, their attempts to spread revolutionary doctrines among the masses of the population had been confined, aside from illegal publications, to either daring demonstrations or furtive meetings, both of which were in constant danger of being broken up by the arrival of police. But in September 1905, the Social-Democratic newspaper *Iskra* urged its followers to seize the newly provided opportunity to get their message across. "Let the hall where the moderate discourse of the professor has been heard in the past from now on ring like a bell with the voice of the revolutionary; in educational institutions let only one science be taught — the science of revolution!"[14]

Few ideas could have brought greater consternation to the liberal professoriate than the thought that their temples of *nauka* should be converted into centers exclusively preoccupied with the *"nauka"* of revolution. At Moscow University, the professors' academic council voted to close the university rather than see it turn into a haven of popular revolutionary activity.[15] But elsewhere the professoriate proved unable or unwilling to resist completely the new development, both because it cautiously sympathized with the revolutionary movement at this stage, and because it quite frankly realized its helplessness, short of the unthinkable recourse to police intervention, in the face of student demands and determination. As a result, compromises between liberal professors and radical students (each of whom had assumed the position of spokesmen for the professoriate and student body as a whole) were reached at several higher educational institutions. At St. Petersburg Polytechnical Institute, for example, professors had threatened to resign *en masse* if students passed a resolution calling for the teaching of the "science of revolution." But the professors went on to resolve that it was the duty of everyone to participate in the "struggle for liberation," so long as this participation did not contradict the seriousness and worth of academic pursuits. Students for their part omitted the offending phrase from their resolution and agreed to resume classes, while at the same time fully proclaiming their right to engage in political activity on campus and to arrange evening lectures on political topics that would be open to the public.[16] A student revolutionary at St. Petersburg University has tersely recalled the terms of the compromise worked out there: "Science in the morning, revolution after dusk."[17]

Public response to the opening of university halls for evening political rallies was overwhelming. In late September and early October the halls of St. Petersburg University were filled with up to ten thousand citizens each evening, and even the relatively isolated Polytechnical Institute regularly drew crowds of two to three thousand. Similar meetings were held at higher educational institutions throughout Russia, although at times in the provinces participants were physically attacked by officially inspired reactionary elements. Orators ranged from student activists to professional revolutionaries having no connection with the educational institution. The importance of these meetings in creating and maintaining the mass revolutionary enthusiasm which sparked the general strike of October 1905 should not be underestimated. Indeed, the establishment of the St. Petersburg Soviet of Workers' Deputies, which held its first meetings on October 13 and 14 in the physics auditorium of the Technological Institute, was a direct by-product of university autonomy.[18]

It was now the government, profoundly alarmed by the turn of events, which earnestly demanded that the universities be closed. In the midst of the general strike, Governor-General D. F. Trepov, autonomy or no autonomy, prohibited further political meetings at St. Petersburg University and insisted that the university officials enforce the ban. The rector pleaded unsuccessfully with students for a temporary closure of the university. Trepov thereupon sent his troops to disperse the next gathering, and several days later (soon after the October Manifesto) the government announced that all higher educational institutions were to be closed until the fall of 1906. This policy was maintained despite sporadic protests by both professors and students.[19]

When classes resumed in the fall of 1906 after an interruption of nearly a year and a half, Russia was still in the grip of extreme political and even revolutionary tension. The First Duma had convened in April 1906, only to be dissolved by the tsar in the following July. Political parties, now legal for the first time in Russian history, engaged in heated oratory as they prepared for the forthcoming January election campaign for the Second Duma. Although with hindsight it is now clear that the tide of revolutionary discontent was ebbing, such a trend was not apparent at the time: bloody peasant revolts continued to erupt throughout the summer, and political terrorists counted some 1600 victims during the course of the year. Government strongman Peter Stolypin responded by declaring a state of emergency and carrying out numerous summary trials and executions of suspected terrorists.

The reassembling of the traditionally volatile student body in this national atmosphere did not augur well for a peaceful resumption of normal academic studies. The continuation of a fragile semi-autonomy for elected university administrators added a new element of delicacy to the situation. The university concessions of August 1905 remained on the books, and a further relaxation was made in the 1884 system of disciplinary supervision over students. The widely detested position of inspector, traditionally filled by a nonuniversity person appointed by the district curator, was replaced by that of prorector, who was to be elected from among the professors by the academic council. By these measures the government had formally relinquished its authority over student disturbances and had finally given in to the professoriate's long-standing insistence that it could handle the problem more effectively than outsiders. Nonetheless, Alexander von Kaufmann (Kaufman), the pragmatic official who now occupied the post of Minister of Education, did not hesitate to instruct university administrators on what was expected of them. In his address to an August 1906 conference of higher education leaders, Kaufmann deplored the long closure of the universities on the grounds that it had deprived the country of badly needed educated personnel. "Dare we hope," he continued,

> that our youth has come to its senses and finally understood that the academy exists for *nauka* and only for *nauka* and that, in the future, institutions of higher education cannot serve as a shelter for political demonstrations, but that they must again become an auditorium for those seeking knowledge; that political disputes, speeches, and resolutions, available now to everyone, must not be allowed to dislodge *nauka* from her temple.[20]

Under normal conditions these words might just as easily have come from the lips of a liberal professor. But in the fall of 1906 one might question whether the professoriate had the ability, or even in some cases the desire, completely to eliminate political activities from university premises. Many professors were embittered by the backtracking of the autocracy since the October Manifesto;[21] the political lull that was temporarily to envelop the country did not begin to set in until late 1907. Equally important was the question of how activist students were to be controlled under conditions in which persuasion was ineffective and recourse to police intervention would be more likely to escalate than curtail the existing tensions. The prevailing attitude of the academic intelligentsia on these problems was expressed by the rector of Kazan University, who journeyed to St. Petersburg in December of 1906 to defend his actions before Kaufmann. Admitting that politics continued to play an active role in the life of the student body, he argued that this was merely a reflection of the political atmosphere in the country as a whole. The important question, he stated, was whether student political activity could be kept from interfering with the proper academic life of the university — a difficult goal which he claimed his administration had achieved during the fall semester. Kaufmann, however, was unimpressed with this report. Educational institutions all over Russia, he charged, were in effect controlled by revolutionary students, who were even demanding the right to participate in the work of the professors' academic councils. It was high time, he stated, for these councils to stand up to the students and to exercise properly the powers of self-government that had been delegated to them.[22]

Kaufmann's charges were not completely wide of the mark. Virtually every higher educational institution in Russia at this time had a central student organ to which representatives were elected on a party basis. Members of the revolutionary parties invariably dominated these organs. Thus, in 1906-7 the central student organ at the St. Petersburg Technological Institute consisted of six Social-Democrats, three Socialist Revolutionaries, and four Kadets; at St. Petersburg University it was dominated by Social-Democrats; at Kiev University it consisted of seven Social-Democrats, seven Socialist Revolutionaries, five Kadets, and four others; while at Kazan University it was composed of six Social-Democrats, five Socialist Revolutionaries, and a lesser number of Kadets.[23] Although the mass public political meetings of the fall of 1905 were not repeated, nonstudents frequently attended the open meetings of the revolutionary parties on campus, and money was regularly collected for illegal revolutionary causes. In addition, student groups continued an earlier practice of blackballing professors holding unpopular political views. During the height of the 1905 crisis, a student *skhodka* at St. Petersburg University had called for the reinstatement of twelve "progressive" professors as well as a boycott of ten "reactionary" ones. At this time a group of liberal professors persuaded the students to retract their action on the grounds that only the academic council had the right to elect professors and that those on the "reactionary" list had not been given a fair hearing. During the following year, however, a student organ headed by the future Bolshevik N. V. Krylenko insisted that a conservative chemist be removed from the list of part-time lecturers, and the academic council acquiesced. In Kazan, students voted to boycott two members of reactionary political groups, one of whom was the university treasurer and the other a professor of law. The academic council, itself a frequent target of abuse from the two individuals, worked out an arrangement whereby students would not be penalized for boycotting them. Although there were no major, prolonged student strikes or demonstrations during 1906–7, the rector of Kiev University subsequently maintained that the student organ during that time made several demands of the university administration, combined with the threat of student disturbances if they were unmet. At Kazan the academic council acquiesced to student demands for the cancellation of classes to protest the trial of two former students for terrorism. Lectures resumed only after the defendants were acquitted.[24]

The government meanwhile was gradually recovering its self-confidence and became determined to reverse some of the political concessions it had granted under pressure during the last two years. In June 1907, Stolypin dispersed the fractious Second Duma and promulgated an unconstitutional unilateral revision of the electoral law for the next Duma. Shortly thereafter, the Council of Ministers issued a ban on student political activity, including in particular central student organs based on representation by political party. Both measures facilitated the government's efforts to recover the initiative from the receding oppositionist and revolutionary forces of society. Instances of professorial protest or student resistance sputtered unconvincingly during 1907–8, while at the beginning of 1908 Kaufmann was replaced by the much more conservative A. N. Schwartz as Minister of Education.

Although one can note a general shift to the right after 1907, professors in different institutions reacted differently. Right-wing professors gained control of the universities in Odessa and Kiev and did not hesitate to call in police in response to student disorders. At Kiev Polytechnic Institute, the faculty was closely divided between the left and the right, but since 1905 it had refused to abide by the Jewish quotas in admitting students. In 1911 three deans were fired by the minister over this issue, and this led to mass resignations of liberal professors. At Moscow University, liberal professors remained in control of the administration but came into continual conflict with student organs. At Kazan University, the liberal (Kadet) rector, who had earned the wrath of the minister for insufficiently zealous actions against student political activity, was reelected, despite articulate opposition from conservative professors, by the academic council in 1909 by a vote of 50-9. The ministry refused to confirm him, and eventually he was replaced by a professor who adhered to the Octobrist party.[25]

Students also reacted divergently to the changing intellectual atmosphere of 1907–14. Some turned to religion, others to pornography and sensual exploits, while still others followed the advice of their professors and concentrated on their studies. The 1907 decree banning student political activity said nothing about nonpolitical student organizations, and for the next decade, groups of this nature flourished on a scale unprecedented before 1905. Many of these groups were devoted to the traditional tasks of organizing student dining halls, libraries, and loan banks, whereas others were devoted to academic, artistic, or religious pursuits. In 1909, at Moscow University alone there were 115 legally recognized student organizations, 77 of which were mutual aid societies. An active student press arose, representing all shades of opinion.[26]

Concerted student activism did not disappear after 1907, but temporarily shifted its emphasis back from political to educational and economic issues. A number of academic measures implemented by Schwartz gave fresh ground for student discontent. Students at Kazan held a strike in the spring of 1908 to protest the decision of the ministry to prohibit women auditors (which many academic councils had authorized since 1906). In the fall of 1908 an academic protest movement was revived in St. Petersburg University and other educational institutions. Student *politiki* were now a minority, but they continued to supply an important current of activism, which regarded the liberal professors as traitors to the cause of true educational and political reform and which sought to capture the leadership of student self-help organizations in order to give them a political as well as an economic orientation.[27]

Before long, the *politiki* were catapulted to the front stage once more. In March 1910 V. M. Purishkevich, a leader of the reactionary Union of Russian People, launched a vehement attack on alleged student revolutionaries from the rostrum of the Third Duma, and later that year the reactionary L. A. Kasso replaced Schwartz as Minister of Education. Gunfire was exchanged between police and students in normally calm New-Russian University.[28] The major confrontation occurred following massive student disorders at the funeral of Leo Tolstoi in November of 1910. Kasso responded with a zeal for police intervention that was unusual even for the tsarist bureaucracy. The result was the expulsion of over three thousand students, the resignation of over a hundred faculty members, and a residue of bitterness and demoralization in Russian universities that lasted until the outbreak of war in 1914.

## THE SEARCH FOR REMEDIES

As Russia entered World War I, therefore, the problem of student activism remained as intractable as ever. After fifty years of countless alternating cycles of concessions and repression, nothing seemed to have been resolved. Indeed, what measures, if any, could have been effective in "solving" the student "problem?" What was the basic cause for the continuing student turmoil? Why did Russian students behave so differently from their counterparts in all other major countries at the time?

Most ministers of education since Dmitri Tolstoi thought they knew the answers to these questions. Their diagnosis remains of interest even though their remedies proved futile. Most student activists, they thought, came from relatively impoverished sectors of the social structure and were insufficiently prepared for serious academic study. The appropriate solution would be to increase the financial costs and academic rigor of higher education.

At first glance, there is a certain plausibility to the hypothesis that the main cause of the continuing tradition of student activism in Russia was a constant influx into the student body of students having a middle- or lower-class background. It was commonly believed among educated Russians in the nineteenth century that the decisive turn in the outlook of the intelligentsia which occurred during the decade of 1856–66 (thereby coinciding with the beginnings of student activism) was the result of a large-scale influx of *raznochintsy,* those of middle- or undetermined-class background, in the ranks of the previously predominantly gentry intelligentsia and student body. Intermittent efforts by the ministry throughout the century to discourage poorer students (such as the increase of tuition from sixty to one hundred rubles per year in 1887[29]) did not on the whole produce the effect desired. With characteristic inconsistency, the ministry simultaneously permitted the expansion of both state- and privately funded tuition rebates and outright stipends to needy students The result was a student body characterized by a high degree of impoverishment. Figures show that from the 1860s to World War I, well over 50 percent of all students were dependent on some form of financial aid.[30] Many students also had to find tutoring or other jobs in order to survive. The percentage of university students who were of noble origin declined from 67 in 1864 to 36 in 1913,[31] and even members of this supposedly elite group were often in financially straitened circumstances. Although precise comparisons are difficult, it is likely that the Russian student body as a whole was considerably more democratic in its social origins than that of other European countries of the time.[32]

Recent research, however, has cast very serious doubts on the hypothesis of a causal correlation between social origins and student radicalism. It cannot readily be demonstrated that the spread of nihilist doctrines and the appearance of student communes in the late fifties and early sixties was accompanied, much less caused, by a sharp change at that time in the social composition of the student body. The fragmentary data more likely suggest that students from the nobility comprised roughly the same percentage of the student body in the 1860s as in the 1840s, and that it was either in the 70s or as early as the 30s or 40s, rather than the 50s or 60s, that the *raznochintsy* first made their numbers felt among the students.[33] Nor were student activists distinguishable on the basis of social origin from the rest of the student body. Brower's sample of radical students in the 1860s and 1870s exhibited virtually the same pattern of social origins as did all university students at that time.[34] Even after 1905, when student political allegiances were divided among the various political parties that had emerged by that time, political orientation was only remotely correlated with student social origins. A recent analysis of a 1909 survey of students at St. Petersburg Technological Institute found that all the major parties drew supporters from noble students, although to be sure the parties of the right and center had a somewhat higher percentage of noble support than those of the left. The anarchists, however, defied even this rather faint pattern by drawing a relatively high percentage of their adherents from students of noble origin.[35]

Thus, both the camaraderie and cohesiveness of outlook that developed within the student body as well as the differences of opinion that remained were largely unrelated to the question of social origin. Students from wealthy noble background tended to abandon their class consciousness when entering the walls of the university. As one historian has put it, "most noblemen then [in the 1870s and 1880s] attending universities were a new breed, who sought higher education as a substitute for their hereditary elite status rather than a reinforcement of it."[36]

If an upper-class background in no sense constituted an immunity against the allure of student activism, impecuniousness, on the other hand, did not guarantee an attraction to radical doctrines. It is true that harsh economic conditions may well have increased frustrations and tensions among Russia's student youth, all the more so in view of the government's frequent harassment of student mutual aid societies. But for many students of humble or impoverished background, the alternative of bearing the hardships and patiently completing the educational requirements so as to receive upon graduation an automatic rank in the state bureaucracy, with its guaranteed upward mobility and job security, seemed a highly preferable alternative to the dangerous path of activism, with its great risks of arrest, permanent expulsion from the university, and exile to remote provincial areas.[37]

What was the attitude of the academic intelligentsia toward the question of the causes and most effective solution to the phenomenon of student activism? Most professors regarded academic turmoil, student strikes, and university closures with undisguised dismay. The divergence of outlook between professors and students is well expressed in an incident which occurred in St. Petersburg during the first student demonstrations of 1861. One professor hurried to the scene to warn students that they were harming the university and the cause of learning. A student quickly retorted, "Who cares about learning [*Chto za nauka*]...! We're deciding vital issues here!"[38]

The 1863 university charter, it will be recalled, placed student discipline in the hands of the academic councils, most of which were quite willing at that time to enforce strict rules. But as the relatively liberal Golovnin was replaced as Minister of Education by Dmitri Tolstoi, and as during the late 1860s and 1870s conflicts sharpened seriously between the autocracy and both students, on the one hand, and the professoriate, on the other, more and more professors came into opposition to the policy of strictly prohibiting student organizations. By 1878 the revolutionary terrorism of the People's Will plus continuing large student demonstrations combined to produce a crisis atmosphere in the halls of both the ministries and the universities. At that time the academic councils of the universities in both Odessa and St. Petersburg sent petitions to the Minister of Education which outlined what was to remain until 1905 the essential basis of the liberal diagnosis of the student problem. The professors completely agreed with the government that the student movement (to say nothing of the revolutionary movement with which it overlapped) was a highly negative phenomenon that should be opposed by preventive measures. Where they disagreed was in their analysis of the causes and the proper solution to the problem. Whereas government figures were inclined to view impoverished and poorly motivated students plus an alleged disciplinary permissiveness on the part of university officials as the chief cause, liberal professors insisted that heavy-handed police surveillance and the prohibition of student organizations were primarily responsible for student disaffection. Only if massive police repressions were avoided and the personal rights and freedoms of students guaranteed, ran the argument of the professors' petitions, would discontent subside and normalcy return to academic halls.[39]

One of the most articulate spokesmen for this point of view was the internationally known chemist N. A. Menshutkin. Menshutkin was widely respected by his colleagues for his administrative abilities and social-political outlook as well as for his scientific accomplishments. In 1887 he resigned his position of dean of the physics-mathematics faculty of St. Petersburg University to protest the actions of an extremely conservative rector who had recently been appointed by the ministry. The rector, who described himself as a loyal servant of the autocracy, had immediately begun to implement the Delianov-Pobedonostsev policies by arbitrarily expelling a number of scholarship students. When students responded with more disorders, he unilaterally dismissed eighty of the demonstrators without consulting either the academic council or the board. Menshutkin thereupon wrote a long memorandum to the minister, in which he argued that such actions only further provoked the students and strengthened the hands of radical leaders. The only way to wean the mass of students away from radical activism, he stated, was to instill in them a respect for the law, which the actions of the rector and the ministry had repeatedly broken, and a respect for *nauka,* without any tendentious overtones.[40]

The Ministry of Education paid only scant and sporadic attention to Menshutkin's advice. His recommendation that some student organizations be legitimized was partially implemented in 1901 as part of a vain attempt to stem the tide of the resurgent student movement.[41] But it was Witte's Ministry of Finance that gave him the opportunity and full authority to implement his proposals by appointing him dean at the soon-to-be-opened St. Petersburg Polytechnical Institute. Asked how the academic life of the new institute could be organized so as to avoid student disorders, he made two major recommendations. First, the office of inspector should be filled by one of the professors rather than an outsider, and the role of the inspector should primarily be that of counselor or adviser to students, rather than that of policeman or disciplinarian. Secondly, courses should be so organized as to foster close faculty-student relations. Lectures should be minimized, and more emphasis placed on laboratory and seminar work requiring independent research by students. If students were inspired with a genuine love of *nauka,* stated Menshutkin, they would be better able to resist the bad influence of the secret circles that were so widespread among Russian youth at the time.[42]

These proposals were accepted, and the Polytechnical Institute did in fact become noted for closer than usual relations between faculty and students. Nonetheless, the contagion of 1904–5 engulfed the institute just as it did virtually all other higher educational institutions in Russia. The conclusion became inescapable that student unrest was not caused primarily by purely academic rules or arrangements, however repressive, but was inextricably linked to broader developments in Russian society as a whole. Menshutkin himself was quick to recognize this fact and to modify his previous position. In late 1904 he authored a resolution adopted by the academic council of the institute which stated that neither strict nor lenient measures had proven effective in quelling student disturbances. They could only be effectively overcome, it continued, by a thorough political reform granting civil rights, freedom of the press, and an elective legislative body.[43] This resolution was adopted at virtually the same time that the newly formed academic union of professors, in which Menshutkin was also active, declared that only a political transformation, not academic autonomy alone in an autocratic system, was capable of ensuring the true development of learning and education.

In retrospect it indeed seems clear that governmental harassment of students, while quite possibly intensifying the nature of student protest during certain periods, was not in itself a primary cause of the student movement. The failure of governmental concessions in the area of student rights to stem the tide of student protest during the 1905 revolution is not the only argument against such an interpretation. It should also be recalled that the years 1855–61, when the first student protest movement developed and many of the enduring thought patterns of student activists were formed, constituted a period of relative leniency on the part of government and university administrators toward the question of student organizations and discipline. The analysis of liberal professors, therefore, who before 1905 singled out government repression of students as the main cause of student activism, seems equally as superficial as that of officials of the Ministry of Education who focused on the influx of middle- and lower-class youth into the student body.

Are we left to agree with the conclusion arrived at by Menshutkin in 1905 that the autocratic political structure itself, with its denial of political and civil rights, was the principal factor in determining the course of student activism? Such a conclusion is partially true, but it omits an important additional dimension: the existence of a distinctive student culture which was handed down from one generation of activists to the next. This culture, closely related to that of the radical intelligentsia as a whole, crystallized in the mid–nineteenth century from the interaction among three factors: the tsarist political system, the elitist and Westernized educational institutions implanted by the Ministry of Education, and Western ideas which spread into Russia. Before long, however, it acquired an independent existence as an autonomous traditional force on its own.

It was during the 1907–14 period that a few members of the intelligentsia began to examine the nature of this student culture and subject it to a sharply critical analysis. The most important critique was written by the liberal A. S. Izgoev and appeared in the 1909 *Vekhi* collection. "University students," he wrote, "are the quintessance of the Russian intelligentsia. For a Russian *intelligent,* it is the highest praise to be called an old student."[44] And indeed, he continued, Russian students before 1905 played a highly positive role by being the only group of educated people who consistently fought for the needs of the whole country rather than thinking only of its own interests. But along with this positive role, the student body consistently exhibited some very serious faults — faults which could be forgiven it before 1905, but which now must be squarely faced. Many of these faults can be traced, argued Izgoev, to the fact that many students, themselves children of members of the rationalist intelligentsia, do not receive any training in positive (or, for Izgoev, religious) values from their parents. The first environment which truly influences them is the underground circle which many pupils join during the last years of their gymnasium study. But these circles, with their disdain for systematic study and enthusiasm for illegal literature, breed an overweening cultural arrogance and narrowness. In the university, the typical student knows very little and studies quite badly, but to the extent that he espouses sufficiently leftist views he is regarded as superior in intellect and insight. Russian student culture is unique among European nationalities by virtue of its intense comradeship and communal life, which keeps the Russian student engaged in a constant whirl of activity. But lacking time either for serious study or serious introspection, the student often finds that upon graduation he has retained nothing of any permanent value. That is why so many graduates accomplish nothing and spend their time wistfully recalling their former roles as student activists. As an antidote, Izgoev recommended that students reject the obsessive aspect of the student ideal of self-sacrifice, and devote themselves instead to "knowledge, industry, and moral restraint."[45]

Izgoev's negative evaluation of student culture was challenged by many of his contemporaries. But more important for our purpose is his premise that many of the characteristics of Russian student activism were determined less by the immediate political and educational policies of the autocracy than by a long-standing mental climate of opinion shared by both student activists and the radical intelligentsia as a whole. Among the main characteristics of this climate of opinion were a strong if vaguely articulated sense of duty to humanity and the Russian people, a hatred of autocracy as constituting a barrier to progress and popular well-being, and a very high regard for both comradely solidarity and the path of individual self-sacrifice.

Russia's Westernized educational institutions played an important role both in creating this climate of opinion in the second third of the nineteenth century and in perpetuating it thereafter. They provided an institutional setting with a hothouse atmosphere in which such sentiments could proliferate and develop among a significant proportion of Russian youth at a particularly impressionable age, and in which they could easily be handed down from one generation to another. In a country already afflicted with numerous anachronistic political and social traditions, they thus helped to create and institutionalize a cultural tradition which also, in time, became impervious to changing external conditions. It was the continuing force of this tradition, combined with continuing political repression, that provided the main impetus behind the recurrent waves of student protest.

It was no doubt inevitable that in a country such as Russia, situated on the edge of European civilization and bearing a basically nonrational indigenous culture, a small group of educated individuals would enthusiastically and uncritically endorse certain Western theories and practices while adopting varying degrees of hostility toward Russian institutions. Tsarist educational policies did not create this problem but, as in the case of the ratio between the primary and higher educational sectors, official actions tended to exacerbate rather than ameliorate the situation. The key decision in this respect was to establish as the most important type of higher educational institution universities devoted to pure learning. This decision had a profound impact on the development of Russian culture in the latter half of the nineteenth century.

James Billington has used a perceptive metaphor when discussing Russian culture during the oppressive reign of Nicholas I: "Like a swollen river suddenly confronted with a major obstacle, the flow was merely diverted into channels that had hitherto carried only a small trickle of ideas. Philosophy, history, and literary criticism replaced politics and religion in the mainstreams of Russian culture."[46] During the second half of the century the "major obstacle" of political censorship continued to exist. But during this time Russian higher education began to provide two new channels — the professorial pursuit of *nauka* and the student activist movement — to help carry some of the cultural overflow. Universities and institutes when transplanted to the environment of autocratic Russia thereby acquired new functions in addition to the typical Western ones of conducting research and selecting and training future professionals and functionaries. They provided cultural and social status for numerous talented individuals who found in the vocation of professor and in the pursuit of *nauka* outlets for deeply held humanitarian impulses which otherwise would have been difficult to satisfy within the confines of the tsarist system. They provided a refuge wherein a potent and influential student culture, despite all the efforts of the autocracy to control it, could find a tenuous security and sustenance that was available nowhere else in Russia.

These unique characteristics of Russian higher education, so fruitful for her cultural life, nonetheless fostered an intellectual climate that was indifferent to the tasks of social and economic development. The academic intelligentsia's unrealistic dream of democratizing Russia by means of the spread of *nauka* contributed to the overemphasis on pure as opposed to applied learning, and on higher as opposed to primary education. The self-righteousness of the student movement valued moral absoluteness and self-sacrifice over the acquisition of knowledge and skills, and encouraged confrontation with the authorities rather than innovative reform efforts within society.

The extent of these attitudes might well have been reduced had both the government and the professoriate looked less to German universities as a model and more to the introduction and broad diffusion among the Russian population of technical education and applied knowledge. Yet the historian is faced with a dilemma in evaluating the possible consequences of this hypothetical alternative. The universities were the cultural nurseries of tsarist Russia, and although reducing their relative importance in the overall educational system might have contributed to a smoother transition to a modern social and economic system, it might also have weakened the foundation of Russia's magnificent cultural and intellectual life. Such a Russia might well have produced fewer Bakunins and Lenins, but also fewer Turgenevs, Tchaikovskys, and Mendeleevs. Would that necessarily have been a good thing?

# CONCLUSION

"I ERECTED A MILL, SO MY SUCCESSORS WILL BE FORCED TO BRING SOME water to it."[1] Such was Peter the Great's response to a contemporary who expressed surprise that he would establish an academy of sciences at a time when the country barely possessed the most rudimentary primary-school system. His successors, however, were to prove extremely slow in supplying the water. Furthermore, the very fact that the mill had been constructed before water was available meant that the entire milling system, so to speak, would be significantly different in Russia than in those countries on which it was ostensibly modeled.

The selective Westernizing reforms of Peter and his successors brought contradictory results in many different areas. Through tremendous efforts he succeeded in fashioning an army that was competitive in the European arena and in constructing a new capital that reflected the latest in Western styles. But the very means he utilized to accomplish these goals — the intensification of the bonds of serfdom, the service requirements of the gentry, and the autocratic power of the tsar — served to make Russia's social structure *less* similar to that of those Western countries he was seeking in part to emulate. While becoming more Western in some respects, Russia was becoming less so in others.[2]

The long-term development of education in Russia exhibits similar characteristics. By the early twentieth century, Russia had joined the front rank of European powers in terms of cultural and scientific achievements, book publishing, and higher education enrollments. Yet the resources which the state was willing to expend on cultural and educational endeavors were strictly limited, with the result that these accomplishments were achieved at the expense of a broader diffusion of education among the population as a whole. Consequently, the very prominence she achieved in some cultural areas helped to prolong a debilitating backwardness in terms of literacy, primary schooling, and vocational skills.

How are we to explain the attraction to both the autocracy and the academic intelligentsia of advanced Western educational models?

Certainly the hankering for prestige and the desire to remove the barbarian image of Russia held by so many Europeans was an important factor in Russian thinking at least as far back as the time of Peter the Great. The military and economic successes of Prussia-Germany in the second half of the nineteenth century undoubtedly heightened the prestige of its educational system in the eyes of Russian officials and academics. Officials furthermore harbored the mistaken belief that strict enforcement of certain aspects of the Prussian system would reduce the incidence of student disaffection in Russia. The very fact that the German system was never instituted in its entirety in Russia and that especially after 1905 an increasing number of senior bureaucrats began openly to criticize some of its basic premises doubtless contributed to its continued attractiveness for the academic intelligentsia. They were able to diagnose Russia's educational ailments as the result of an incomplete adoption of the German model, rather than to confront the possibility that the model itself may have been inappropriate.

One can sympathize with the best representatives of tsarist officialdom and the liberal professoriate as they grappled with the problem of how to mold an educational system that would contribute to the modernization and cohesion of a country so immense and diverse. Members of each group brought to bear on the problem an inherited set of values, assumptions, and constraints which had developed historically in the Russian context, but which handicapped them by limiting the nature of the alternatives they could perceive or recommend. A few individuals, such as Sergei Witte and Paul Ignatiev on the one hand, or Vladimir Vernadskii on the other, probed the limits of some of these inherited assumptions, and displayed a willingness to adopt a more flexible approach. But we are left to conclude that on the whole both the autocracy and the academic intelligentsia were mistaken in the prescriptions they provided for Russia's educational problems.

Indeed, the peculiar nature and structure of the Russian educational system must be counted as one of the many factors contributing to both the collapse of tsardom and the failure of the Provisional Government in 1917. To be sure, the relationship between formal education and either political stability or social cohesion is an elusive subject. Nonetheless, some informed speculation, based on the conclusions of the foregoing analysis, would seem warranted. The most obvious factor to consider is the role of higher educational institutions in spawning continuing numbers of student activists and radical drop-outs. Although students qua students rarely constituted an immediate danger to the regime — their demonstrations could always be suppressed with troops if necessary — many who earned their spurs in student activism went on to become propagandists among the people and leaders of the revolutionary underground.

It is perhaps more important to consider the impact of the educational system on the much larger number of graduates who, while moving into respected positions in society rather than joining the parties of the revolutionary left, nevertheless adopted an oppositionist attitude toward the autocratic system. More often than not the never-ceasing efforts of the bureaucracy to subject all students to control and surveillance and to forbid them to form student organizations led to a lasting resentment toward autocratic power. Even those who did not become student activists frequently sympathized with the plight of their comrades and found themselves influenced by the prevailing atmosphere of the student culture in most schools.

There were of course many students, on the other hand, who turned out exactly as the authorities wished them to be — loyal to the autocracy, hard-working, and dedicated. The Imperial Lyceum, School of Jurisprudence, and military academies seem to have been particularly successful at producing this type of graduate, but the number of products of seminaries, institutes, and universities who faithfully followed the career opportunities open to them should not be underestimated. Yet even here one might ask if the type of education provided was the most appropriate for the interests of the autocracy. Too often the nature of the curriculum reinforced the propensity of the intelligentsia to think in abstract rather than practical terms and to dwell on Western theories rather than Russian realities. In short, the educational system as a whole seems to have done much less than it might have to provide its graduates with the self-reliance and persistence to work for piecemeal reform, or with the first-hand knowledge and insight needed to cope with the staggering social and economic problems of late Imperial Russia.

Finally, it is important to consider the types of people who were *not* educated, owing to the peculiar structure of the system. The funneling of scarce educational resources into select secondary and higher educational institutions actually served to widen the gap between the elite and *narod,* a gap which liberal rhetoric was impotent to bridge and which proved so devastating to political stability during 1917. The high degree of illiteracy among the soldiers, the shortage of skilled workers among the labor force, and the paucity of secondary-level technicians in all areas of the economy undoubtedly made an important contribution to the economic and military breakdown of Russia in World War I.

A remark attributed to Witte accurately sums up the dilemma faced by tsarist education officials: "Education foments social revolution, but popular ignorance loses wars." The predicament was unenviable, and in the final analysis, tsarism failed to cope with it. We may conclude that the autocracy succeeded only in impaling itself on *both* horns of the dilemma: it provided enough education to foment a revolution, but not enough to avoid losing a war.

# NOTES

### INTRODUCTION

1. Alexandra, Empress of Russia, *Letters of the Tsaritsa to the Tsar, 1914-1916* (New York, 1924), pp. 393-94.

2. For a discussion of this issue, see Georges Florovsky, "The Problem of Old Russian Culture," and the ensuing debate, reprinted in Donald W. Treadgold, ed., *The Development of the USSR: An Exchange of Views* (Seattle, 1964), pp. 125-72.

3. For a concise definition and analysis of the term "intelligentsia;" see Martin Malia, "What Is the Intelligentsia?" in Richard Pipes, ed., *The Russian Intelligentsia* (New York, 1961), pp. 1-18. Historians disagree concerning how broadly or narrowly the term should be defined. (Cf., for example, L. K. Erman, "Sostav intelligentsii v Rossii v kontse XIX i nachale XX v." [The composition of the intelligentsia in Russia at the end of the 19th and beginning of the 20th century], *Istoriia SSSR* [History of the USSR], no. 1 [1963], pp. 161-77; and Michael Confino, "On Intellectuals and Intellectual Traditions in Eighteenth- and Nineteenth-Century Russia," *Daedalus* 101 [Spring 1972]: 117-49.) I use the term in a relatively broad but subjective sense, in which the most important component is a feeling of moral obligation to strive for a more ideal society in Russia. As such, the intelligentsia as a whole is composed of a number of constituent groups: a classical intelligentsia (members of the first generation of the thirties and forties), a radical intelligentsia, a liberal intelligentsia, and even a conservative intelligentsia (including the Slavophiles and *pochvenniki*). The academic intelligentsia is a subgroup of the liberal intelligentsia. For a further explanation and justification of the term "academic intelligentsia," see part 2, esp. p. 65.

### INTRODUCTION TO PART ONE

1. William H. E. Johnson, *Russia's Educational Heritage* (1950; New York, 1964); Nicholas Hans, *History of Russian Educational Policy, 1701-1917* (1931; New York, 1964); Paul Miliukov, *Ocherki po istorii russkoi kul'tury* [Sketches in the history of Russian culture], Jubilee edition, 3 vols. (Paris, 1930-37), vol. 2, part 2 (1931). Two recent works are much more sophisticated in their approach, but remain basically critical of tsarist educational practice before 1900: Patrick L. Alston, *Education and the State in Tsarist Russia* (Stanford, 1969); Allen Sinel, *The Classroom and the Chancellery: State*

*Educational Reform in Russia under Count Dmitry Tolstoi* (Cambridge, Mass., 1973).

2. Nicholas S. Timasheff, *The Great Retreat: The Growth and Decline of Communism in Russia* (New York, 1946), p. 39.

3. See the remarks by George F. Kennan and Hugh Seton-Watson in Richard Pipes, ed., *Revolutionary Russia* (Cambridge, Mass., 1968), pp. 5, 16-18.

4. Alston, p. 248.

CHAPTER ONE

1. Marc Raeff, *Origins of the Russian Intelligentsia: The Eighteenth Century Nobility* (New York, 1966), pp. 132-33. I shall translate the term *dvorianstvo* interchangeably as either "nobility" or "gentry." For some observations on the imprecision of either translation, see Raeff, pp. 8-9.

2. Miliukov, *Ocherki,* p. 739. Unless otherwise stated, all translations from the Russian are my own.

3. Allen A. Sinel, "The Socialization of the Russian Bureaucratic Elite, 1811-1917: Life at the Tsarskoe Selo Lyceum and the School of Jurisprudence," *Russian History* 3, no. 1 (1976): 1-31; James H. Billington, *The Icon and the Axe: An Interpretive History of Russian Culture* (New York, 1966), p. 188; Robert E. Jones, *The Emancipation of the Russian Nobility, 1762-1785* (Princeton, 1973), pp. 67-71.

4. A. A. Kizevetter, "Istoricheskii ocherk" [Historical sketch] in V. B. El'iashevich et al., *Moskovskii Universitet, 1755-1930: Iubileinyi sbornik* [Moscow University, 1755-1930: Jubilee collection] (Paris, 1930), pp. 13-16; Alexander Vucinich, *Science in Russian Culture: A History to 1860* (Stanford, 1963), pp. 131-35. This Vucinich volume will hereafter be cited as Vucinich I.

5. James T. Flynn, "V. N. Karazin, the Gentry, and Kharkov University," *Slavic Review* 28, no. 2 (1969): 209-20.

6. Alston, pp. 87-96; Sinel, *The Classroom and the Chancellery,* pp. 141-50.

7. The women students, however, were separated from the men and, with very few exceptions, were granted only the highly restricted degree of advanced midwife (*uchenaia akusherka*). The experiment ended soon after 1882, when General P. S. Vannovskii replaced Miliutin as Minister of War. See Christine Johanson, "Autocratic Politics, Public Opinion, and Women's Medical Education during the Reign of Alexander II, 1855-1881," *Slavic Review* vol. 38, no. 3 (September 1979).

8. Alston, pp. 86, 154.

9. Ibid., p. 124.

10. A. Kireev, "O predstoiashchei reforme nashego obrazovaniia" [On the forthcoming reform of our education] *Russkii Vestnik* [Russian herald], January 1902, p. 317.

11. During this 115-year period there were 34 ministers of the interior, 27 ministers of education, 23 ministers of transportation, 21 ministers of justice, 19 ministers of war, 18 ministers of finance, and 15 ministers of foreign affairs. Erik Amburger, *Geschichte der Behördenorganisation Russlands von Peter dem*

*Grossen bis 1917* (Leiden, 1966), pp. 136-37, 192, 266, 171, 298, 208, 130.

12. For two recent studies of this problem, see Daniel R. Brower, *Training the Nihilists: Education and Radicalism in Tsarist Russia* (Ithaca, N.Y., 1975); Alain Besançon, *Éducation et société en Russie dans le second tiers du xix^e siècle* (Paris, 1974).

13. Quoted in Billington, p. 293. For two different interpretations of Magnitskii, see Billington, 290-96, and James T. Flynn, "Magnitskii's Purge of Kazan University: A Case Study in the Uses of Reaction in Nineteenth-Century Russia," *Journal of Modern History* 43 (1971): 598-614.

14. Alston, pp. 98-101.

15. For a table showing the number of weekly hours devoted to various subjects by each grade of the Tolstoi gymnasium, see Hans, *History of Russian Educational Policy,* p. 118.

16. Alston, p. 153.

17. The quotation is from Pushkin's character Eugene Onegin, who lamented that the nobility picked up its education "in bits and pieces, something and somehow." The phrase was subsequently used by reformers, both liberal and conservative, to show the need for more comprehensive academic curricula in the school systems. See Alston, pp. 66-67, 82-83. For Tolstoi's use of the expression and his argument that his brand of classicism avoids the pitfall by requiring an intense amount of work and self-discipline, see Ministerstvo Narodnago Prosveshcheniia, *Zhurnal* [Journal] (hereafter *Zhurnal*), 182, no. 11-12, section 4 (1875): 67-68.

18. Sinel, *The Classroom and the Chancellery,* pp. 176-78, 199-200.

19. *Zhurnal,* 182, no. 11-12, sec. 4 (1875): 131-32.

20. P. A. Zaionchkovskii, *Rossiiskoe samodershavie v kontse XIX stoletiia* [The Russian autocracy at the end of the 19th century] (Moscow, 1970), pp. 309-10.

21. Konstantin P. Pobedonostsev, *Reflections of a Russian Statesman* (Ann Arbor, 1965), pp. 75-84.

22. On Pobedonostsev's reestablishment of the church system, see Miliukov, *Ocherki,* pp. 832-34. For enrollment data, see A. Rashin, "Gramotnost' i narodnoe obrazovanie v Rossii v XIX i nachale XX v." [Literacy and public education in Russia in the 19th and beginning of the 20th centuries], *Istoricheskie zapiski* [Historical notes] 37 (1951): 61-65.

23. *Tekhnologicheskii Institut imeni Leningradskogo Soveta: Sto let, 1828-1928* [The Leningrad Soviet Technological Institute: One hundred years, 1828-1928], 2 vols. (Leningrad, 1928), 1: 94-95, 100-103.

24. On the political motivation, see Hans, *History of Russian Educational Policy,* pp. 151-54. For details on Vyshnegradskii's plan and the nature of the schools established, see A. N. Veselov, *Professional'no-tekhnicheskoe obrazovanie v SSSR: Ocherki po istorii srednego i nizshego proftekhobrazovaniia* [Vocational-technical education in the USSR: Studies in the history of secondary and primary vocational-technical education] (Moscow, 1961), pp. 9-17; and "Professional'noe obrazovanie" [Vocational education], in F. A. Brockhaus [*Brokgauz*] and I. A. Efron, *Entsiklopedicheskii slovar'* [Brockhaus-Efron

encyclopedia], vol. 25A (50) (St. Petersburg, 1898), pp. 568-74.

25. The data I have used came from Rashin, pp. 69-74. For an original treatment of this issue, see Alston, pp. 120-39.

26. Miliukov, *Ocherki*, pp. 693-704; Billington, pp. 127-29; Max J. Okenfuss, "The Jesuit Origins of Petrine Education," in J. G. Garrard, ed., *The Eighteenth Century in Russia* (New York, 1973), pp. 106-30.

27. For a description of these schools, see Max J. Okenfuss, "Technical Training in Russia under Peter the Great," *History of Education Quarterly* 13 (Winter 1973): 325-45.

28. Miliukov, *Ocherki*, p. 733.

29. Walter M. Pintner, "The Social Characteristics of the Early Nineteenth-Century Russian Bureaucracy," *Slavic Review* 29, no. 3 (September 1970): 429-43; Walter M. Pintner, "The Russian Higher Civil Service on the Eve of the 'Great Reforms,'" *Journal of Social History* (Spring 1975), pp. 55-68; Harold A. McFarlin, "The Extension of the Imperial Russian Civil Service to the Lowest Office Workers: The Creation of the Chancery Clerkship, 1827-1833," *Russian History* 1, pt. 1 (1974): 1-17.

30. Quoted by K. A. Timiriazev, "Probuzhdenie estestvoznaniia v tret'ei chetverti veka" [The awakening of natural science in the third quarter of the century], in Russkii Bibliograficheskii Institut Granat, *Istoriia Rossii v XIX veke* ]The Granat history of Russia in the 19th century], 9 vols. (St. Petersburg, 1907-11), 7: 2.

31. "Voprosy zhizni" [Questions of life], originally published in *Morskoi sbornik* [Maritime journal] (1856). Head of the Naval Department at that time was Grand Duke Constantine, who was sympathetic to reform sentiments. The article is reprinted in N. I. Pirogov, *Izbrannye pedagogicheskie sochineniia* [Selected pedagogical works] (Moscow, 1952), pp. 55-84.

32. Paul Miliukov, "Universitety v Rossii" [Universities in Russia], in Brockhaus and Efron, *Entsiklopedicheskii slovar'*, vol. 34A (68) (St. Petersburg, 1902), p. 791.

33. Pirogov, pp. 121-24.

34. Alston, pp. 202-3.

35. S. P. Timoshenko, "The Development of Engineering Education in Russia," *Russian Review* 15, no. 3 (1956): 173-77; *Tekhnologicheskii Institut imeni Leningradskogo Soveta,* 1:11-16, 64; Walter M. Pintner, *Russian Economic Policy under Nicholas I* (Ithaca, 1967), pp. 48-52, 232.

36. Kireev, pp. 305, 317.

37. Quoted by Arcadius Kahan in C. Arnold Anderson and Mary Jean Bowman, eds., *Education and Economic Development* (Chicago, 1965), pp. 4-5.

38. Quoted by Vucinich I, p. 74. On Peter's attitude toward science and the establishment of the academy, see ibid., pp. 43-48, 65-74; Miliukov, *Ocherki*, pp. 744-46; and V. N. Tatishchev, "Razgovor o pol'ze nauk i uchilishch" [Conversation on the utility of the sciences and schools], in Obshchestvo Istorii i Drevnostei Rossiiskikh pri Moskovskom Universitete, *Chteniia* [Readings], 1887, bk. 1, sec. 1, pp. 1-171.

39. Vucinich I, pp. 97-98.

40. *Zhurnal,* 145, sec. 4 (September 1869): 2.

41. Loren R. Graham, *The Soviet Academy of Sciences and the Communist Party, 1927-1932* (Princeton, 1967), p. 9.

42. Cf. Alexander Vucinich, *Science in Russian Culture, 1861-1917* (Stanford, 1970), pp. 66-73, which presents a more positive view of the academy. This volume will hereafter be cited as Vucinich II.

43. Richard Pipes, ed. and trans., *Karamzin's Memoir on Ancient and Modern Russia: A Translation and Analysis* (Cambridge, Mass., 1959), pp. 158-59.

44. Ibid., pp. 160-61.

45. For a description of the pitiful state of affairs at Kazan University even before the appointment of Magnitskii as curator, see Flynn, "Magnitskii's Purge of Kazan University."

46. Friedrich Paulsen, *The German Universities and University Study,* trans. F. Thilly and W. Elwang (London, 1906), pp. 332-51.

47. Ministerstvo Narodnago Prosveshcheniia, *Trudy Vysochaishe Uchrezhdennoi Komissii po Preobrazovaniiu Vysshykh Uchebnykh Zavedenii* [Works of the Imperial Commission on the Reform of Higher Educational Institutions], vol. 3 (St. Petersburg, 1903), pp. 10-11, 76-85.

48. Sinel, *The Classroom and the Chancellery,* pp. 131-32, 166-67.

49. *Zhurnal,* 182, no. 11-12, sec. 4 (1875): 67-68.

50. K. D. Ushinskii, *Izbrannye pedagogicheskie sochineniia* [Selected pedagogical works], 2 vols. (Moscow, 1953-54), 2: 250-51, 268-69 (first quotation), 264, 278 (second quotation, emphasis in original).

## CHAPTER TWO

1. The entire manifesto is translated and included as an appendix in Alston, pp. 260-66. The quotation is on p. 263.

2. Ibid., p. 261.

3. Oskar Anweiler, *Geschichte der Schule und Pädagogik in Russland vom Ende des Zarenreiches bis zum Beginn der Stalin-Ära* (Berlin, 1964), pp. 42-48. Anweiler stresses both the heavy dependency of Russian pedagogical thought of the early twentieth century on Western progressives and the impact this trend had subsequently on early Soviet education.

4. Paul N. Ignatiev, Dimitry M. Odinetz, and Paul J. Novgorotsev, *Russian Schools and Universities in the World War,* Economic and Social History of the World War: Russian Series (New Haven, 1929), p. xxii.

5. Quoted by N. A. Konstantinov, *Ocherki po istorii srednei shkoly: Gimnazii i real'nye uchilishcha s kontsa XIX v. do Fevral'skoi Revoliutsii 1917 g.* [Sketches in the history of the secondary school: Gymnasia and realschulen from the end of the 19th century to the February Revolution of 1917], 2d ed. (Moscow, 1956), p. 94.

6. Sir Bernard Pares, *Russia between Reform and Revolution,* ed. Francis B. Randall (1907; New York, 1962), p. 184. For an example of liberal criticism against the ministry, see the series of articles on higher education written by Vladimir I. Vernadskii, which appeared in *Ezhegodnik gazety Rech'* [Yearbook

of the newspaper *Rech'*]: "1911 god v istorii russkoi umstvennoi kul'tury [The year 1911 in the history of Russian intellectual culture] (1912), pp. 323-41; "Vysshaia shkola i nauchnyia organizatsii" [The higher school and scientific organizations] (1913), pp. 351-71; "Vysshaia shkola v Rossii" [The higher school in Russia] (1914), pp. 308-25.

7. See Table 4 in Hans, *History of Russian Educational Policy,* p. 232.

8. "Ustav o sluzhbe po opredeleniiu ot Pravitel'stva" [Statute on the civil service], *Polnyi svod zakonov rossiiskoi imperii* [The complete code of laws of the Russian Empire], ed. A. A. Dobrovol'skii, 16 vols. (St. Petersburg, 1911), vol. 3, bk. 1, arts. 3-8, 40, 48-132.

9. Ignatiev et al., pp. 29-30.

10. Alston, p. 205.

11. Vucinich II, pp. 211-12.

12. Alston, pp. 229-31.

13. On Shaniavskii University, see A. A. Kizevetter, *Na rubezhe dvukh stoletii* (*vospominaniia, 1881-1914*) [On the border of two centuries (memoirs, 1881-1914)] (Prague, 1929), pp. 470-95.

14. J. L. Black, "Educating Women in Eighteenth Century Russia: Myths and Realities," *Canadian Slavonic Papers* 20, no. 1 (March 1978): 23-43.

15. Sophie Satina, *Education of Women in Pre-Revolutionary Russia* (New York, 1966), p. 41.

16. Ibid., pp. 61-62.

17. Enrollment data from Rashin, pp. 69-76. See also Alston, pp. 203-4, and Satina, passim. There were, of course, in addition a sizeable number of boys enrolled in commercial, technical, and other vocationally oriented schools.

18. J. M. Meijer, *Knowledge and Revolution: The Russian Colony in Zuerich* (*1870-1875*) (Assen, 1955), esp. pp. 23-25; *Vysshie zhenskie* (*Bestuzhevskie*) *kursy: Bibliograficheskii ukazatel'* [Women's higher (Bestuzhev) courses: Bibliographical guide] (Moscow, 1966), p. 8.

19. Elena Likhacheva, *Materialy dlia istorii zhenskago obrazovaniia v Rossii, 1856-1880* [Materials for a history of women's education in Russia, 1856-1880] (St. Petersburg, 1901), pp. 493-535.

20. Ibid., pp. 593-618.

21. Johanson, "Autocratic Politics."

22. Satina, pp. 104-6.

23. Ibid., pp. 93, 137.

24. Ibid., p. 135.

25. There were 33,489 women students in 1914-15, 35,700 university students in 1913, and a total of 109,937 students in the 81 out of 97 higher educational institutions for which enrollment data is available for 1914-15. *Trudy Tsentral'nogo Statisticheskogo Upravleniia* [Works of the Central Statistical Administration], 35 vols. (Moscow, 1920-28), vol. 28, pt. 1, *Narodnoe obrazovanie v SSSR* [Public education in the USSR] (1926), pp. 518-19. University enrollment data from Rashin, p. 77.

26. A leading contemporary specialist on the development of women's edu-

cation, for example, pointed out that in the areas of higher and secondary education for women, Russian accomplishments either equalled or surpassed those of all other European countries. Concerning girls' elementary schooling, however, Russia occupied one of the lowest ranks on the European scale. (Likhacheva, 646-47.) Although specifically referring to the early 1880s, these statements are undoubtedly true for the years before World War I as well.

27. Ignatiev et al., pp. 8-14.

28. Rashin (p. 68) calculates that 51 percent of school age children were enrolled as of January 1, 1915. Regional variations ranged from 1.9 percent in Samarkand *oblast'* to 78.2 percent in Tula *guberniia*.

29. For a summary of Kasso's primary school policy, see Ignatiev et al., pp. 20-24.

30. For changes in the gymnasium, see Alston, pp. 140-71, and Miliukov, *Ocherki,* pp. 836-37.

31. Data are from Alston, p. 209, and Rashin, pp. 69-75.

32. The information, but not the interpretation, has been taken primarily from Alston, pp. 208-20.

33. N. V. Speranskii, *Krizis russkoi shkoly: Torzhestvo politicheskoi reaktsii: Krushenie universitetov* [The crisis of the Russian school: The triumph of political reaction: The destruction of the universities] (Moscow, 1914), pp. 109-12, 122-27. For a list of those who resigned their positions, see *Russkie Vedomosti* [Russian gazette], 20 February 1911, p. 2.

34. Samuel D. Kassow, "The Russian University in Crisis, 1899-1911" (Ph.D. diss., Princeton University, 1976), p. 619; Vladimir I. Vernadskii, "Vysshaia shkola v Rossii," pp. 309-11.

35. D. I. Bagalei, "Ekonomicheskoe polozhenie russkikh universitetov," [The economic condition of Russian universities], *Vestnik Evropy* [Herald of Europe], (January 1914), pp. 222-24.

36. Rashin, p. 77. This figure does not include women who were enrolled in university-level women's higher courses.

37. Bagalei, p. 222; Vucinich II, pp. 201-2.

38. Vucinich II, p. 213.

39. *Tekhnologicheskii Institut imeni Leningradskogo Soveta,* 1: 119.

40. Bagalei, pp. 222-53.

41. Alston, p. 286.

42. Hans, *History of Russian Educational Policy,* p. 229. If the educational expenditures of the other central ministries are included, the educational portion amounted to 7.2 percent of the state budget (ibid., p. 230). In addition, there were considerable outlays by public organizations and private individuals.

43. Alston, pp. 205, 286.

44. Rashin, pp. 69-75; Hans, *History of Russian Educational Policy,* pp. 182-85, 210, 237.

45. According to one calculation, the proportion of all higher education students who were studying at commercial institutes increased from .9 percent in 1907 to 6.4 percent in 1914. See table 6. See also A. F. Fortunatov, "O

vysshem kommercheskom obrazovanii [On higher commercial education], in Fortunatov, *Po voprosam nauchnoi shkoly* [Issues concerning the academic school] (Moscow, 1916), pp. 23-34.

46. Gregory Guroff, "The Legacy of Pre-Revolutionary Economic Education: St. Petersburg Polytechnic Institute," *Russian Review*, July, 1972, pp. 272-85; Leon Smolinski, "Grinevetskii and Soviet Industrialization," *Survey*, April 1968, pp. 100-115.

47. *S-Peterburgskii Politekhnicheskii Institut Imperatora Petra Velikogo, 1902-1952* [St. Petersburg Polytechnical Institute in the name of Emperor Peter the Great, 1902-1952], 2 vols. (Paris-New York, 1952-58), 1: 40-42, 2: 56-59; Theodore H. Von Laue, *Sergei Witte and the Industrialization of Russia* (New York, 1963), p. 221.

48. *S-Peterburgskii Politekhnicheskii Institut*, 1: 7-10, 17-20, 42; Stephen P. Timoshenko, *As I Remember: The Autobiography of Stephen P. Timoshenko*, trans. Robert Addis (Princeton, 1968), pp. 79-83.

49. Sir Bernard Pares, *The Fall of the Russian Monarchy* (New York, 1939), p. 411. See also Leonid I. Strakhovsky, "Count P. N. Ignat'yev, Reformer of Russian Education," *Slavonic and East European Review* 36, no. 86 (December 1957): 1-26.

50. Ignatiev et al., pp. 97-100.

51. Anweiler, p. 37.

52. Ignatiev et al., pp. xx-xxi.

53. Ibid., pp. 110-13.

54. Ibid., p. xxiv.

55. Anweiler, pp. 41-42.

56. Ignatiev et al., pp. 196-97.

57. For a comparative statistical analysis of nineteenth-twentieth century education and economic systems which supports this point, although it does not include Russia or the Soviet Union, see Michael Kaser, "Education and Economic Progress: Experience in Industrialized Market Economies," in E. A. G. Robinson and J. Vaizey, eds., *The Economics of Education* (London, 1966), pp. 89-173.

58. Gregory Guroff and S. Frederick Starr, "A Note on Urban Literacy in Russia, 1890-1914," *Jahrbücher für Geschichte Osteuropas* 19 (December 1971): 520-31, esp. 525; Carlo M. Cipolla, *Literacy and Development in the West* (Baltimore, 1969), p. 129.

59. Maurice Friedberg, *Russian Classics in Soviet Jackets* (New York, 1962), pp. ix, 177. See also Guroff and Starr, pp. 527-28.

60. Joseph Ben-David, "The Growth of the Professions and the Class System," in Reinhard Bendix and Seymour M. Lipset, eds., *Class, Status and Power*, 2d ed. (New York, 1966), p. 464.

### INTRODUCTION TO PART TWO

1. N. V. Shelgunov, L. P. Shelgunova, M. L. Mikhailov, *Vospominaniia* [Memoirs], 2 vols. (Moscow, 1967), 1: 93-94.

2. Quoted by I. N. Borozdin, "Universitety v Rossii v epokhu 60-kh godov"

[Universities in Russia during the period of the 1860s], Russkii Bibliograficheskii Institut Granat, *Istoriia Rossii v XIX veke* [The Granat history of Russia
in the 19th century], 9 vols. (St. Petersburg, 1907-11) 4: 189-90.

3. Vucinich II, p. 34.

4. Ibid., pp. 19-20.

5. Timiriazev, "Probuzhdenie estestvoznaniia v tret'ei chetverti veka," 7: 29.

CHAPTER THREE

1. My estimate is based on a doubling of the figures for universities alone as of
January 1, 1912, as provided in Ministerstvo Narodnago Prosveshcheniia,
*Vsepoddaneishii otchet za 1911* [Most loyal report for 1911] (St. Petersburg,
1913), appendix, pp. 2-3. Although university students constituted only one-
third of the total student body at this time, I have doubled rather than tripled
the number of university personnel because many professors and privatdocents
held more than one teaching position.

2. G. I. Shchetinina, *Universitety v Rossii i ustav 1884 goda* [Universities in
Russia and the charter of 1884] (Moscow, 1976), pp. 49-50.

3. Vucinich II, pp. 201-2.

4. A. S. Lappo-Danilevsky, "The Development of Science and Learning in
Russia," in J. D. Duff, ed., *Russian Realities and Problems* (Cambridge, 1917),
pp. 173-74.

5. Vucinich II, pp. 68, 215.

6. Ibid., pp. 96-98; V. I. Modestov, "Russkaia nauka v poslednie dvadtsat'
piat' let" [Russian science during the last twenty-five years], *Russkaia Mysl'*
[Russian thought] no. 5 (1890), pp. 73-91.

7. M. N. Pokrovskii, "Reforma vysshei shkoly" [Reform of the higher school],
*Narodnoe Prosveshchenie: Ezhenedel'noe prilozhenie k Izvestiiam* [Public
education: Weekly appendix to *Izvestiia*], July 20, 1918.

8. Vucinich II, pp. 324-27.

9. On the accomplishments of Russian scholars and scientists, see ibid.,
passim; Alexander Vucinich, *Social Thought in Tsarist Russia: The Quest for
a General Science of Society, 1861-1917* (Chicago, 1976), esp. pp. 125-72;
Judith E. Zimmerman, "Sociological Ideas in Pre-Revolutionary Russia,"
*Canadian-American Slavic Studies* 9 (Fall 1975): 302-23; Pitirim Sorokin,
"Russian Sociology in the Twentieth Century," *American Sociological Society:
Papers and Proceedings,* 21 (1927): 57-69.

10. Vucinich II, pp. 362-82.

11. Ibid., pp. 356-61; Timoshenko, "The Development of Engineering Education in Russia," p. 177.

12. V. R. Leikina-Svirskaia, *Intelligentsiia v Rossii vo vtoroi polovine XIX
veka* [The intelligentsia in Russia during the second half of the 19th century]
(Moscow, 1971), p. 184.

13. Marc Raeff, *Origins of the Russian Intelligentsia,* pp. 117-18.

14. Leikina-Svirskaia, pp. 177-78; Shchetinina, pp. 50-52, 169-70, 184-87.
The latter author's claim that there was a significant increase of nonnoble
professors as a result of the 1884 charter is not supported by her own data.

15. M. M. Kovalevskii, "Moskovskii Universitet v kontse 70-ikh i nachale 80-ikh godov proshlogo veka," [Moscow University at the end of the 70s and beginning of the 80s of the last century], *Vestnik Evropy* [Herald of Europe], April, 1910, pp. 185-87.

16. A. A. Kizevetter, *Na rubezhe dvukh stoletii,* pp. 21-22.

17. B. N. Menshutkin, *Zhizn' i deiatel'nost' Nikolaia Aleksandrovicha Menshutkina* [The life and work of Nicholas Alexandrovich Menshutkin] (St. Petersburg, 1908), pp. 189-99, 212-13; Kassow, "The Russian University in Crisis," pp. 318-23, 335-45, 462-68.

18. George Fischer, *Russian Liberalism: From Gentry to Intelligentsia* (Cambridge, Mass., 1958), pp. 140-41.

19. William G. Rosenberg, *Liberals in the Russian Revolution: The Constitutional Democratic Party, 1917-1921* (Princeton, 1974), pp. 20-21, 24.

20. Menshutkin, pp. 293-95.

21. M. K. Korbut, *Kazanskii Gosudarstvennyi Universitet im. V. I. Ul'ianova-Lenina za 125 let, 1804/05-1929/30* [The V. I. Ul'ianov-Lenin Kazan State University during the course of 125 years, 1804/05-1929/30], 2 vols. (Kazan, 1930), 2: 235-36, 279.

22. Fritz K. Ringer, *The Decline of the German Mandarins: The German Academic Community, 1890-1933* (Cambridge, Mass., 1969), pp. 102-13.

23. K. A. Timiriazev, "Nauka" [Science], in Russkii Bibliograficheskii Institut Granat, *Entsiklopedicheskii slovar'* [Encyclopedia Granat], 7th ed. (Moscow, n.d.), vol. 30, cols. 1-53.

24. Vladimir Solov'ev, "Nauka," in F. A. Brockhaus [*Brokgauz*] and I. A. Efron, *Entsiklopedicheskii slovar'* [Brockhaus-Efron encyclopedia], vol. 20A (40) (St. Petersburg, 1897), p. 692.

25. D. N. Ovsianiko-Kulikovskii, "Psikhologiia russkoi intelligentsii" [The psychology of the Russian intelligentsia], *Intelligentsiia v Rossii: Sbornik statei* [The intelligentsia in Russia: Collection of articles] (St. Petersburg, 1910), p. 195.

26. Rosenberg, p. 13.

27. For a positive view of professorial oppositionist activity between 1884 and the end of the century, see Shchetinina, pp. 164-88.

28. Much of this declaration is reprinted in Menshutkin, pp. 190-91.

29. For an example of reactionary polemics on the subject, see Vladimir Purishkevich, *Materialy po voprosu o razlozhenii sovremennago russkago universiteta* [Materials on the question of the corruption of the contemporary Russian university] (St. Petersburg, 1914).

30. N. A. Berdiaev, "Filosofskaia istina i intelligentskaia pravda" [Philosophical truth-wisdom as opposed to the intelligentsia's truth-justice], in *Vekhi: Sbornik statei o russkoi intelligentsii* [Signposts: A collection of articles on the Russian intelligentsia] (Moscow, 1909), p. 8.

31. Ibid., pp. 6-11.

32. Ovsianiko-Kulikovskii, pp. 192-219.

33. V. A. Mikhel'son, "Rasshirenie i natsional'naia organizatsiia nauchnykh izsledovanii v Rossii" [The expansion and national organization of scientific

research in Russia], *Priroda* [Nature] no. 5-6 (1916), cols. 696-98.

34. F. M. Friche, "Vysshaia shkola v kontse veka" [The higher school at the end of the century], Russkii Bibliograficheskii Institut Granat, *Istoriia Rossii v XIX veke,* 9 vols. (St. Petersburg, 1907-11), 9:153-54. For another report of similar student sentiments, see P. G. Vinogradov, "Uchebnoe delo v nashikh universitetakh" [The academic system in our universities], *Vestnik Evropy* [Herald of Europe], no. 5 (October 1901), p. 539.

35. *Put' studenchestva: Sbornik statei* [The path of the student body: A collection of articles] (Moscow, 1916), p. 64. Italics in original.

36. Ibid., pp. 80-81.

## CHAPTER FOUR

1. A. V. Nikitenko, *The Diary of a Russian Censor,* abridged, ed., and trans. Helen Saltz Jacobson (Amherst, 1975), p. 240.

2. A. V. Nikitenko, *Moia povest' o samom sebe i o tom, "chemu svidetel' v zhizni byl'":* *Zapiski i dnevnik (1804-1877 gg.)* [My story about myself and about all that I witnessed during my life: Notes and diary (1804-1877)], 2 vols. 2d ed. (St. Petersburg, 1904-5), 1:590. For more comments against democracy in Russia, see ibid., 2:157-58.

3. Ibid., 1:194.

4. Ibid., 1:495.

5. Ibid., 1:380-81.

6. Ibid., 1:389.

7. Ibid., 1:552.

8. Ibid., 1:628; 2:6, 36-37, 61.

9. Ibid., 2:31-32.

10. Ibid., 2:213. Emphasis in original.

11. Ibid., 2:140, 182; Nikitenko, *Diary,* p. 286.

12. N. V. Speranskii, *Krizis,* pp. 1-12.

13. Ibid., pp. 34-39, 102.

14. Ibid., pp. 40-45.

15. Ibid., p. 112.

16. Frederic Lilge, *The Abuse of Learning: The Failure of the German University* (New York, 1948); Ringer, passim; Joseph Ben-David and Awraham Zloczower, "Universities and Academic Systems in Modern Societies," *Archives européennes de sociologie* 3 (1962): 45-84.

17. Friedrich Paulsen, pp. 79-86. The author, a firm believer in academic freedom and autonomy, gives a qualified endorsement to the right of the states to overrule the universities with regard to appointments, as well as to the prohibition of Social Democrats from holding professorial posts. See also pp. 246-52.

18. Quoted in Ringer, p. 143.

19. Ben-David and Zloczower, for example, argue that German scientific excellence stemmed from the decentralized and competitive nature of the university system in the first half of the century rather than from its internal structure or the philosophical ideas on which it was presumably based.

20. K. A. Timiriazev, *Nauka i demokratiia: Sbornik statei, 1904-1919 gg* [Science and democracy: A collection of articles, 1904-1919] (Moscow, 1963), pp. 37-39. I have used the 1963 edition of this work because a spot check indicated that there are no significant differences between it and the first edition, published immediately after the author's death in 1920.

21. Ibid., pp. 11-12.

22. Ibid., p. 43. Italics in original.

23. Ibid., pp. 379-80. For an impassioned defense of the proposition that science has no need of any philosophy above or beyond itself, see *Nasushchnye zadachi sovremennogo estestvoznaniia* [The urgent tasks of contemporary natural science], in Timiriazev, *Sochineniia* [Works], 10 vols. (Moscow, 1937-40), 5: 17-18.

24. Vucinich II, pp. 275-89. For strong attacks on Weismann in 1895 and 1890, see Timiriazev, *Sochineniia,* 5: 32, 139. For a more qualified but still skeptical appraisal of Weismann in 1905 and Mendel in 1909, see Timiriazev, *Sochineniia,* 5: 318, and Timiriazev, *Nauka i demokratiia,* pp. 159-61.

25. Timiriazev, *Nauka i demokratiia,* pp. 315-28.

26. Ibid., p. 15.

27. See Timiriazev, *Sochineniia,* 5: 17 (first published 1904), where he argues that the most urgent task of science is to combat reactionary philosophy in all of its manifestations.

28. Timiriazev, *Nauka i demokratiia,* pp. 52-54.

29. Ibid., pp. 17-18, 32-35.

30. Quotation in ibid., p. 19. For Pirogov's views on the relation between social opinion and university autonomy and on universities as barometers of society, see Pirogov, *Izbrannye pedagogicheskie sochineniia,* pp. 411-12, 454. For Timiriazev's support of early Bolshevik efforts to reform the universities, see Timiriazev, *Nauka i demokratiia,* 414-20.

31. Timiriazev, *Nauka i demokratiia,* p. 49; Timiriazev, *Sochineniia,* 5: 25-26.

32. Paulsen, pp. 117-19; Ben-David and Zloczower, p. 59. Paulsen, writing in the first years of the twentieth century, noted and welcomed a recent change in this attitude among German academics, some of whom adopted social attitudes and responsibilities similar to those of their Russian counterparts. Still, those whom Ringer has labelled the "Orthodox Mandarins" resisted efforts to democratize the educational system well into the twentieth century. See Ringer, pp. 282-95, and Paulsen, pp. 125-31.

33. M. M. Kovalevskii, pp. 179-81.

34. V. I. Vernadskii, *Ocherki i rechi* [Sketches and speeches], 2 vols. (Petrograd, 1922) 1:3-25, 145-58; Vucinich II, pp. 395-96, 413-16. On the desperate efforts to create a chemical industry during wartime, see Vladimir N. Ipatieff, *The Life of a Chemist: Memoirs of Vladimir N. Ipatieff* (Stanford, 1946), pp. 190-240.

35. Timiriazev, *Nauka i demokratiia,* pp. 56-66; Vucinich II, pp. 211-13.

36. Timiriazev, *Nauka i demokratiia,* pp. 424-52. Lazarev was elected to the Academy of Sciences in 1917 and went on to become a prominent Soviet

physicist. For his account of the founding of the Physics Institute, see P. P. Lazarev, *Ocherki istorii russkoi nauki* [Sketches in the history of Russian science] (Moscow-Leningrad, 1950), pp. 72-74, 221-22.

37. G. V. Vernadskii, "Bratstvo 'Priiutino'" [The Brotherhood of Shelter] *Novyi Zhurnal* [New journal] 93 (1968): 147-71; ibid. 95 (1969): 202-15; ibid. 96 (1969): 153-71; ibid. 97 (1969): 218-37. I am indebted to Kendall E. Bailes for this reference.

38. Vucinich II, pp. 479-80.

39. V. I. Vernadskii, *Pis'ma o vysshem obrazovanii v Rossii* [Letters on higher education in Russia] (Moscow, 1913), p. 4.

40. Ibid., pp. 5-6.

41. Ibid., pp. 8-9.

42. V. I. Vernadskii, "Vysshaia shkola i nauchnyia organizatsii" [The higher school and scientific organizations], *Ezhegodnik gazety Rech' na 1913 god* [Yearbook of the newspaper *Rech'* for 1913] (St. Petersburg, 1913), p. 370.

43. Ibid., pp. 368-71; V. I. Vernadskii, "Vysshaia shkola v Rossii" [The higher school in Russia], *Ezhegodnik gazety Rech' na 1914 god* (St. Petersburg, 1914), p. 308.

44. V. I. Vernadskii, *Pis'ma o vysshem obrazovanii,* pp. 9-15, 19.

45. V. I. Vernadskii, "Vysshaia shkola v Rossii," pp. 310-11.

46. Kizevetter, *Na rubezhe,* p. 31.

47. Ibid., pp. 169-71.

48. Ibid., pp. 286-305.

49. Ibid., pp. 296-97.

50. The St. Petersburg and Moscow committees on literacy, to which academics as well as other public figures had devoted considerable time and energy, were deprived of their autonomy and in effect destroyed by government decrees in 1895 and 1896. See ibid., pp. 228-41. The Sunday-school movement, though it revived later in the century, had expired in 1862 as the result of internal weakness and governmental intervention. See Reginald E. Zelnik, *Labor and Society in Tsarist Russia: The Factory Workers of St. Petersburg, 1855-1870* (Stanford, 1971), pp. 173-95.

51. Kizevetter, *Na rubezhe,* p. 298.

52. "Svod ustavov uchenykh uchrezhdenii i uchebnykh zavedenii vedomstva Ministerstva Narodnago Prosveshcheniia" [Code of charters of research establishments and academic institutions under the jurisdiction of the Ministry of Public Education], *Svod zakonov rossiiskoi imperii* [Code of laws of the Russian Empire], vol. 11, pt. 1, app. to the note of art. 397.

53. Kizevetter, *Na rubezhe,* pp. 490-93.

54. "Svod ustavov," app. to the note of art. 397.

55. Kizevetter, *Na rubezhe,* p. 484.

56. Ibid., p. 484. For N. V. Speranskii's views on this issue, see Speranskii, *Bor'ba za shkolu: Iz proshlago i nastoiashchago na Zapade i v Rossii* [The struggle for the school: From the past and the present in the West and in Russia] (Moscow, 1910), pp. 182-92.

57. Kizevetter, *Na rubezhe,* pp. 267-68.

CHAPTER FIVE

1. William L. Mathes, "University Courts in Imperial Russia," *Slavonic and East European Review,* July 1974, p. 371.

2. L. Martov, P. Maslov, and A. Potresov, eds., *Obshchestvennoe dvizhenie v Rossii v nachale XX-go veka* [The social movement in Russia at the beginning of the 20th century], 4 vols. (St. Petersburg, 1909-14), 1: 263; Menshutkin, p. 51.

3. Martov et al., 1: 275.

4. William L. Mathes, "The Origins of Confrontation Politics in Russian Universities: Student Activism, 1855-1861," *Canadian Slavic Studies* 2 (Spring 1968): 28-45.

5. Sinel, pp. 94-95; Mathes, "University Courts," pp. 375-76.

6. *Tekhnologicheskii Institut imeni Leningradskogo Soveta: Sto let, 1828-1928* [The Leningrad Soviet Technological Institute: One hundred years, 1828-1928], 2 vols. (Leningrad, 1928), 1: 63, 73-74, 86-87.

7. Friche, pp. 146-47.

8. Mathes, "University Courts," p. 380.

9. Daniel R. Brower, *Training the Nihilists,* pp. 197-208.

10. Friche, pp. 155-58; Martov et al., 1: 264-67.

11. Samuel D. Kassow, however, has argued persuasively that the student movement was never controlled by the political parties, even when its leaders vociferously proclaimed their party allegiance (Kassow, esp. pp. 231-53, 263-65, 725). This is the best work in any language on the student movement.

12. V. V. Mavrodin, ed., *Istoriia Leningradskogo Universiteta, 1819-1969; Ocherki* [Sketches in the history of Leningrad University, 1819-1969] (Leningrad, 1969), pp. 153-57; V. I. Lenin, "Zadachi revoliutsionnoi molodezhi" [The tasks of revolutionary youth] (first pub. 1903), in *Lenin o narodnom obrazovanii* [Lenin on public education] (Moscow, 1957), pp. 49-60; Menshutkin, pp. 56-68, 73-77; Korbut, 2: 184-97; Martov et al., 1: 273-83.

13. Mavrodin, pp. 161-64; Menshutkin, pp. 185-89, 194.

14. Quoted in Menshutkin, p. 199.

15. Kassow, pp. 406-12.

16. Menshutkin, pp. 200-201.

17. W. S. Woytinsky, *Stormy Passage: A Personal History through Two Russian Revolutions to Democracy and Freedom, 1905-1960* (New York, 1961), p. 29.

18. *Tekhnologicheskii Institut imeni Leningradskogo Soveta,* 1:284.

19. Woytinsky, pp. 32-36; Mavrodin, pp. 168-70; Menshutkin, pp. 212-13.

20. Quoted in Korbut, 2: 236.

21. An expression of this sentiment can be seen in the replacement by Kazan University professors in early 1907 of an Octobrist slate of deputies to the State Council by a Kadet slate. Ibid., 2: 279.

22. Ibid., pp. 241-42.

23. *Tekhnologicheskii Institut imeni Leningradskogo Soveta,* 1:289; Ipatieff, pp. 144-46; *Put' studenchestva,* p. 22; Korbut, 2: 244.

24. Korbut, 2: 237-38, 244-45; Woytinsky, pp. 27-29; Ipatieff, pp. 144-46; *Put' studenchestva*, p. 23.

25. Timoshenko, *As I Remember*, pp. 116-17; *Put' studenchestva*, pp. 122, 127; Korbut, 2: 258-59, 263.

26. *Put' studenchestva*, pp. 25-27; Ignatiev et al., pp. 142-45.

27. V. I. Lenin, "Studencheskoe dvizhenie i sovremennoe politicheskoe polozhenie" [The student movement and the contemporary political situation] (first pub. 1908), in *Lenin o narodnom obrazovanii*, pp. 79-84; Korbut, 2: 253-58; *Put' studenchestva*, passim.

28. Speranskii, *Krizis*, pp. 99-105.

29. Shchetinina, p. 195.

30. L. V. Kamosko, "Izmeneniia soslovnogo sostava uchashchikhsia srednei i vysshei shkoly Rossii (30-80-e gody XIX v.)" [Changes in the estate composition of students in secondary and higher schools in Russia (1830s-80s)], *Voprosy istorii* [Questions of history], no. 10 (1970), p. 204; Alston, p. 155; Friche, p. 145; Shchetinina, pp. 73-75; Ignatiev et al., pp. 141-42.

31. A. Rashin, pp. 77-78.

32. For some additional comments on this point, as well as an estimated breakdown of the social composition of all higher education students in the Russian Empire as of 1914, see James C. McClelland, "Proletarianizing the Student Body: The Soviet Experience during the New Economic Policy," *Past & Present*, no. 80 (August 1978), pp. 135-38.

33. Brower, *Training the Nihilists*, pp. 41-68, 110-16; Michael Confino, p. 129; Alan P. Pollard, "The Russian Intelligentsia: The Mind of Russia," *California Slavic Studies* 3 (1964): 26-27. Soviet historians avoid the issue. Both Shchetinina (pp. 70-72) and Kamosko (p. 204) present data for university students' social origins in the 1850s and 1870s, omitting data for the 1860s. Rashin (pp. 77-78) presents data for the 1860s (in which students from the nobility comprise roughly the same percentage as in Shchetinina's and Kamosko's data for the 1850s) but not for the 1850s or 1870s. Shchetinina virtually admits (p. 75) that students from the nobility played a disproportionate role in the student movement, although she rightly points out that many noble students were financially hard-pressed.

34. Brower, *Training the Nihilists*, p. 44.

35. Daniel R. Brower, "Student Political Attitudes and Social Origins: The Technological Institute of Saint Petersburg," *Journal of Social History*, Winter 1972-73, pp. 202-13.

36. Vucinich II, p. 60.

37. Shchetinina, p. 75.

38. Nikitenko, *Diary*, p. 232.

39. Shchetinina, pp. 66-67.

40. Menshutkin, pp. 33-47.

41. Ibid., pp. 73-75; Korbut, 2: 187-88.

42. Menshutkin, pp. 153-54.

43. Reprinted in ibid., pp. 178-79.

44. A. S. Izgoev, "Ob intelligentnoi molodezhi" [On the youth of the intelligentsia], in *Vekhi,* p. 105.

45. Ibid., pp. 97-124. Quotation on p. 116.

46. Billington, p. 308.

## CONCLUSION

1. Tatishchev, p. 110.

2. This theme has been developed by Alexander Gerschenkron in his *Economic Backwardness in Historical Perspective: A Book of Essays* (Cambridge, Mass., 1962), pp. 5-30.

# SELECTED BIBLIOGRAPHY

The following list does not include all works consulted or cited, but only those that are of the most significance for the topics considered in this book.

Alston, Patrick L. *Education and the State in Tsarist Russia.* Stanford, 1969.

Amburger, Erik. *Geschichte der Behördenorganisation Russlands von Peter dem Grossen bis 1917.* Leiden, 1966.

Anderson, C. Arnold, and Bowman, Mary Jean, eds. *Education and Economic Development.* Chicago, 1965.

Anweiler, Oskar. *Geschichte der Schule und Pädagogik in Russland vom Ende des Zarenreiches bis zum Beginn der Stalin-Ära.* Berlin, 1964.

Bagalei, D. I. "Ekonomicheskoe polozhenie russkikh universitetov" [The economic condition of Russian universities]. *Vestnik Evropy* [Herald of Europe], January 1914, pp. 222-53.

Ben-David, Joseph. "The Growth of the Professions and the Class System." In Reinhard Bendix and Seymour M. Lipset, eds., *Class, Status and Power,* pp. 459-72. 2d ed. New York, 1966.

——, and Zloczower, Awraham. "Universities and Academic Systems in Modern Societies." *Archives européennes de sociologie* 3 (1962): 45-84.

Berdiaev, N. A. "Filosofskaia istina i intelligentskaia pravda" [Philosophical truth-wisdom as opposed to the intelligentsia's truth-justice]. In *Vekhi: Sbornik statei o russkoi intelligentsii* [Signposts: A collection of articles on the Russian intelligentsia], pp. 1-22. Moscow, 1909.

Besançon, Alain. *Éducation et société en Russie dans le second tiers du xix^e siècle.* Paris, 1974.

Billington, James H. *The Icon and the Axe: An Interpretive History of Russian Culture.* New York, 1966.

Black, Cyril E. *The Dynamics of Modernization: A Study in Comparative History.* New York, 1966.

Black, J. L. "Educating Women in Eighteenth Century Russia: Myths and Realities." *Canadian Slavonic Papers* 20, no. 1 (March 1978): 23-43.

Borozdin, I. N. "Universitety v Rossii v epokhu 60-kh godov" [Universities in Russia during the period of the 1860s]. In Russkii Bibliograficheskii Institut Granat, *Istoriia Rossii v XIX veke* [The Granat history of Russia in the 19th century], 9 vols. (St. Petersburg, 1907-11), 4: 185-212.

Brower, Daniel R. "Student Political Attitudes and Social Origins: The Technological Institute of Saint Petersburg." *Journal of Social History,* Winter 1972-73, pp. 202-13.

———. *Training the Nihilists: Education and Radicalism in Tsarist Russia.* Ithaca, N.Y., 1975.

Cipolla, Carlo M. *Literacy and Development in the West.* Baltimore, 1969.

Confino, Michael. "On Intellectuals and Intellectual Traditions in Eighteenth- and Nineteenth-Century Russia." *Daedalus* 101 (Spring 1972): 117-49.

Dzhanshiev, G. A. *Epokha velikikh reform* [The epoch of the great reforms]. 10th ed. St. Petersburg, 1907.

Eimontova, R. G. "Universitetskii vopros i russkaia obshchestvennost' v 50-60-kh godakh XIX veka" [The university question and Russian public opinion in the 50s and 60s of the 19th century]. *Istoriia SSSR* [History of the USSR], no. 6 (1971), pp. 144-58.

Erman, L. K. "Sostav intelligentsii v Rossii v kontse XIX i nachale XX v." [The composition of the intelligentsia in Russia at the end of the 19th and beginning of the 20th century]. *Istoriia SSSR* [History of the USSR], no. 1 (1963), pp. 161-77.

Famintsyn, A. S. "Nakanune universitetskoi reforme" [On the eve of university reform]. *Mir Bozhii* [God's world], January 1903, pp. 238-55.

Florovsky, Georges. "The Problem of Old Russian Culture." Reprinted in Donald W. Treadgold, ed., *The Development of the USSR: An Exchange of Views,* pp. 125-72. Seattle, 1964.

Flynn, James T. "Magnitskii's Purge of Kazan University: A Case Study in the Uses of Reaction in Nineteenth-Century Russia." *Journal of Modern History* 43 (1971): 598-614.

———. "V. N. Karazin, the Gentry, and Kharkov University." *Slavic Review* 28, no. 2 (1969): 209-20.

Fortunatov, A. F. *Po voprosam nauchnoi shkoly* [Issues concerning the academic school]. Moscow, 1916.

Friche, F. M. "Vysshaia shkola v kontse veka" [The higher school at the end of the century]. In Russkii Bibliograficheskii Institut Granat, *Istoriia Rossii v XIX veke* [The Granat history of Russia in the 19th century], 9 vols. (St. Petersburg, 1907-11), 9: 145-63.

Gerschenkron, Alexander. *Economic Backwardness in Historical Perspective: A Book of Essays.* Cambridge, Mass., 1962.

Guroff, Gregory. "The Legacy of Pre-Revolutionary Economic Education: St. Petersburg Polytechnic Institute." *Russian Review,* July 1972, pp. 272-85.

———, and Starr, S. Frederick, "A Note on Urban Literacy in Russia, 1890-1914." *Jahrbücher für Geschichte Osteuropas* 19 (December 1971): 520-531.

Hans, Nicholas. *History of Russian Educational Policy, 1701-1917.* 1931; New York, 1964.

———. *The Russian Tradition in Education.* London, 1963.

Ignatiev, Paul N., Odinetz, Dimitry M., and Novgorotsev, Paul J. *Russian Schools and Universities in the World War.* Economic and Social History of the World War: Russian Series. New Haven, 1929.

Ipatieff, Vladimir N. *The Life of a Chemist: Memoirs of Vladimir N. Ipatieff.*

Ed. by X. J. Eudin, H. D. Fisher, and H. H. Fisher. Trans. by V. Haensel and R. Lusher. Stanford, 1946.

*Istoriia Moskovskogo Universiteta* [History of Moscow University]. 2 vols. Moscow, 1955.

Izgoev, A. S. "Ob intelligentnoi molodezhi" [On the youth of the intelligentsia]. In *Vekhi: Sbornik statei o russkoi intelligentsii* [Signposts: A collection of articles on the Russian intelligentsia], pp. 97-124. Moscow, 1909.

Johanson, Christine. "Autocratic Politics, Public Opinion, and Women's Medical Education during the Reign of Alexander II, 1855-1881." *Slavic Review* 38, no. 3 (September 1979).

Johnson, William H. E. *Russia's Educational Heritage.* 1950; New York, 1964.

Kamosko, L. V. "Izmeneniia soslovnogo sostava uchashchikhsia srednei i vysshei shkoly Rossii (30-80-e gody XIX v.)" [Changes in the estate composition of students in secondary and higher schools in Russia (1830s-80s)]. *Voprosy istorii* [Questions of history] no. 10 (1970), pp. 203-7.

Kaser, Michael. "Education and Economic Progress: Experience in Industrialized Market Economies." In E. A. G. Robinson and J. Vaizey, eds., *The Economics of Education,* pp. 89-173. London, 1966.

——. "Education in Tsarist And Soviet Development." In C. Abramsky, ed., *Essays in Honour of E. H. Carr,* pp. 229-54. London, 1974.

Kassow, Samuel D. "The Russian University in Crisis, 1899-1911." Ph.D. dissertation. Princeton University, 1976.

Kireev, A. "O predstoiashchei reforme nashego obrazovaniia" [On the forthcoming reform of our education]. *Russkii Vestnik* [Russian herald], January 1902, pp. 303-31.

Kizevetter, A. A. "Istoricheskii ocherk" [Historical sketch]. In V. B. El'iashevich et al., *Moskovskii Universitet, 1755-1930: Iubileinyi sbornik* [Moscow University, 1755-1930: Jubilee collection], pp. 9-140. Paris, 1930.

——. *Na rubezhe dvukh stoletii (vospominaniia, 1881-1914)* [On the border of two centuries (memoirs, 1881-1914)]. Prague, 1929.

——. "O sbornike 'Vekhi'" [On the "Vekhi" collection]. *Russkaia Mysl'* [Russian thought] 30 (May 1909): 127-37.

Konstantinov, N. A. *Ocherki po istorii srednei shkoly: Gimnazii i real'nye uchilishcha s kontsa XIX v. do Fevral'skoi Revoliutsii 1917 g.* [Sketches in the history of the secondary school: Gymnasia and realschulen from the end of the 19th century to the February Revolution of 1917]. 2d ed. Moscow, 1956.

Korbut, M. K. *Kazanskii Gosudarstvennyi Universitet imeni V. I. Ul'ianova-Lenina za 125 let, 1804/05-1929/30* [The V. I. Ul'ianov-Lenin Kazan State University during the course of 125 years, 1804/05-1929/30]. 2 vols. Kazan, 1930.

Kovalevskii, M. M. "Moskovskii Universitet v kontse 70-ikh i nachale 80-ikh godov proshlogo veka" [Moscow University at the end of the 70s and beginning of the 80s in the last century]. *Vestnik Evropy* [Herald of Europe], April, 1910, pp. 178-221.

Lappo-Danilevsky, A. S. "The Development of Science and Learning in

Russia." In J. D. Duff, ed., *Russian Realities and Problems,* pp. 153-229. Cambridge, 1917.

Leikina-Svirskaia, V. R. *Intelligentsiia v Rossii vo vtoroi polovine XIX veka* [The intelligentsia in Russia during the second half of the 19th century]. Moscow, 1971.

Lenin, V. I. "Studencheskoe dvizhenie i sovremennoe politicheskoe polozhenie" [The student movement and the contemporary political situation] (first pub. 1908). In *Lenin o narodnom obrazovanii* [Lenin on public education], pp. 79-84. Moscow, 1957.

———. "Zadachi revoliutsionnoi molodezhi" [The tasks of revolutionary youth] (first pub. 1903). In *Lenin o narodnom obrazovanii* [Lenin on public education], pp. 49-60. Moscow, 1957.

Likhacheva, Elena. *Materialy dlia istorii zhenskago obrazovaniia v Rossii, 1856-1880* [Materials for a history of women's education in Russia, 1856-1880]. St. Petersburg, 1901.

McFarlin, Harold A. "The Extension of the Imperial Russian Civil Service to the Lowest Office Workers: The Creation of the Chancery Clerkship, 1827-1833." *Russian History* 1, pt. 1 (1974): 1-17.

Malia, Martin. "What Is the Intelligentsia?" In Richard Pipes, ed., *The Russian Intelligentsia,* pp. 1-18. New York, 1961.

Martov, L., Maslov, P., and Potresov, A., eds. *Obshchestvennoe dvizhenie v Rossii v nachale XX-go veka* [The social movement in Russia at the beginning of the 20th century]. 4 vols. St. Petersburg, 1909-14.

Mathes, William L. "N. I. Pirogov and the Reform of University Government, 1856-1866." *Slavic Review* 31 (March 1972): 29-51.

———. "The Origins of Confrontation Politics in Russian Universities: Student Activism, 1855-1861." *Canadian Slavic Studies* 2 (Spring 1968): 28-45.

———. "University Courts in Imperial Russia." *Slavonic and East European Review,* 52, no. 128 (July 1974): 366-81.

Mavrodin, V. V., ed. *Istoriia Leningradskogo Universiteta, 1819-1969; Ocherki* [Sketches in the history of Leningrad University, 1819-1969]. Leningrad, 1969.

Meijer, J. M. *Knowledge and Revolution: The Russian Colony in Zuerich (1870-1875).* Assen, 1955.

Menshutkin, B. N. *Zhizn' i deiatel'nost' Nikolaia Aleksandrovicha Menshutkina* [The life and work of Nicholas Alexandrovich Menshutkin]. St. Petersburg, 1908.

Mikhel'son, V. A. "Rasshirenie i natsional'naia organizatsiia nauchnykh izsledo-vanii v Rossii" [The expansion and national organization of scientific research in Russia]. *Priroda* [Nature] no. 5-6 (1916), cols. 679-98.

Miliukov, Paul. *Ocherki po istorii russkoi kul'tury* [Sketches in the history of Russian culture]. Jubilee edition, 3 vols. Paris, 1930-37.

———. "Universitety v Rossii" [Universities in Russia]. In F. A. Brockhaus [*Brokgauz*] and I. A. Efron, *Entsiklopedicheskii slovar'* [Brockhaus-Efron encyclopedia], vol. 34A (68) (St. Petersburg, 1902), pp. 788-800.

Ministerstvo Narodnago Prosveshcheniia. *Trudy Vysochaishe Uchrezhdennoi*

*Komissii po Preobrazovaniiu Vysshikh Uchebnykh Zavedenii* [Works of the Imperial Commission on the Reform of Higher Educational Institutions], vol. 3. St. Petersburg, 1903.

——. *Vsepoddaneishii otchet Ministra Narodnago Prosveshcheniia* [Most loyal report of the Minister of Public Education]. St. Petersburg, 1841, 1907-13.

——. *Zhurnal* [Journal]. St. Petersburg. Vols. 1-362 (1834-1905); vols. 1-72 (1906-17).

Modestov, V. I. "Russkaia nauka v poslednie dvadtsat' piat' let" [Russian science during the last twenty-five years]. *Russkaia Mysl'* [Russian thought] no. 5 (1890), pp. 73-91.

Monroe, Paul, ed. *A Cyclopedia of Education.* 5 vols. New York, 1911-12.

Nikitenko, A. V. *The Diary of a Russian Censor.* Abridged, and trans. by Helen Saltz Jacobson. Amherst, 1975.

——. *Moia povest' o samom sebe i o tom, "chemu svidetel' v zhizni byl'"*: *Zapiski i dnevnik,* (*1804-1877 gg.*) [My story about myself and about all that I witnessed during my life: Notes and diary (1804-1877)]. 2 vols. 2d ed. St. Petersburg, 1904-5.

Okenfuss, Max J. "The Jesuit Origins of Petrine Education." In J. G. Garrard, ed., *The Eighteenth Century in Russia,* pp. 106-30. New York, 1973.

——. "Technical Training in Russia under Peter the Great." *History of Education Quarterly* 13 (Winter 1973): 325-45.

Ovsianiko-Kulikovskii, D. N. "Psikhologiia russkoi intelligentsii" [The psychology of the Russian intelligentsia]. *Intelligentsiia v Rossii: Sbornik statei* [The intelligentsia in Russia: Collection of articles], pp. 192-219. St. Petersburg, 1910.

Pares, Sir Bernard. *Russia between Reform and Revolution.* Ed. by Francis B. Randall. 1907; New York, 1962.

Paulsen, Friedrich. *The German Universities and University Study.* Trans. by F. Thilly and W. Elwang. London, 1906.

Pintner, Walter M. "The Russian Higher Civil Service on the Eve of the 'Great Reforms.'" *Journal of Social History,* Spring 1975, pp. 55-68.

——. "The Social Characteristics of the Early Nineteenth-Century Russian Bureaucracy." *Slavic Review* 29, no. 3 (September 1970): 429-43.

Pipes, Richard. "The Historical Evolution of the Russian Intelligentsia." In Richard Pipes, ed., *The Russian Intelligentsia,* pp. 47-62. New York, 1961.

——, ed. and trans. *Karamzin's Memoir on Ancient and Modern Russia: A Translation and Analysis.* Cambridge, Mass., 1959.

Pirogov, N. I. *Izbrannye pedagogicheskie sochineniia* [Selected pedagogical works]. Moscow, 1952.

Pobedonostsev, Konstantin P. *Reflections of a Russian Statesman.* Ann Arbor, 1965.

Pollard, Alan P. "The Russian Intelligentsia: The Mind of Russia." *California Slavic Studies* 3 (1964): 1-32.

*Polnyi svod zakonov rossiiskoi imperii* [The complete code of laws of the Russian Empire]. 16 vols. Ed. by A. A. Dobrovol'skii. St. Petersburg, 1911.

"Professional'noe obrazovanie" [Vocational education]. In F. A. Brockhaus

[*Brokgauz*] and I. A. Efron, *Entsiklopedicheskii slovar'* [Brockhaus-Efron encyclopedia], vol. 25A (50) (St. Petersburg, 1898), pp. 563-74.

*Put' studenchestva: Sbornik statei* [The path of the student body: A collection of articles]. Moscow, 1916.

Raeff, Marc. *Origins of the Russian Intelligentsia: The Eighteenth-Century Nobility.* New York, 1966.

Rashin, A. "Gramotnost' i narodnoe obrazovanie v Rossii v XIX i nachale XX v." [Literacy and public education in Russia in the 19th and beginning of the 20th centuries]. *Istoricheskie zapiski* [Historical notes] 37 (1951): 28-80.

Riasanovsky, Nicholas V. *A Parting of Ways: Government and the Educated Public in Russia, 1801-1855.* Oxford, 1976.

Ringer, Fritz K. *The Decline of the German Mandarins: The German Academic Community, 1890-1933.* Cambridge, Mass., 1969.

Rozhdestvenskii, S. V. *Istoricheskii obzor deiatel'nosti Ministerstva Narodnago Prosveshcheniia, 1802-1902* [Historical survey of the activity of the Ministry of Public Education]. St. Petersburg, 1902.

*Russkie Vedomosti* [Russian gazette]. Moscow, 1864-1918.

*S-Peterburgskii Politekhnicheskii Institut Imperatora Petra Velikogo, 1902-1952* [St. Petersburg Polytechnical Institute in the name of Emperor Peter the Great, 1902-1952]. 2 vols. Paris-New York, 1952-58.

Satina, Sophie. *Education of Women in Pre-Revolutionary Russia.* New York, 1966.

Shchetinina, G. I. *Universitety v Rossii i ustav 1884 goda* [Universities in Russia and the charter of 1884]. Moscow, 1976.

Sinel, Allen. *The Classroom and the Chancellery: State Educational Reform in Russia under Count Dmitry Tolstoi.* Cambridge, Mass., 1973.

——. "The Socialization of the Russian Bureaucratic Elite, 1811-1917: Life at the Tsarskoe Selo Lyceum and the School of Jurisprudence." *Russian History* 3, no. 1 (1976): 1-31.

Smolinski, Leon. "Grinevetskii and Soviet Industrialization." *Survey,* April 1968, pp. 100-115.

Solov'ev, Vladimir. "Nauka" [Science]. In F. A. Brockhaus [*Brokgauz*] and I. A. Efron, *Entsiklopedicheskii slovar'* [Brockhaus-Efron encyclopedia], vol. 20A (40) (St. Petersburg, 1897), p. 692.

Sorokin, Pitirim. "Russian Sociology in the Twentieth Century." *American Sociological Society: Papers and Proceedings* 21 (1927): 57-69.

Speranskii, N. V. *Bor'ba za shkolu: Iz proshlago i nastoiashchago na Zapade i v Rossii* [The struggle for the school: From the past and the present in the West and in Russia]. Moscow, 1910.

——. *Krizis russkoi shkoly: Torzhestvo politicheskoi reaktsii: Krushenie universitetov* [The crisis of the Russian school: The triumph of political reaction: The destruction of the universities]. Moscow, 1914.

Strakhovsky, Leonid I. "Count P. N. Ignat'yev, Reformer of Russian Education." *Slavonic and East European Review,* 36, no. 86 (December 1957): 1-26.

Tatishchev, V. N. "Razgovor o pol'ze nauk i uchilishch" [Conversation on the utility of the sciences and schools]. In Obshchestvo Istorii i Drevnostei Rossiiskikh pri Moskovskom Universitete, *Chteniia* [Readings], 1887, bk. 1, section 1, pp. 1-171.

*Tekhnologicheskii Institut imeni Leningradskogo Soveta: Sto let, 1828-1928* [The Leningrad Soviet Technological Institute: One hundred years, 1828-1928]. 2 vols. Leningrad, 1928.

Timasheff, Nicholas S. *The Great Retreat: The Growth and Decline of Communism in Russia.* New York, 1946.

Timiriazev, K. A. *Nasushchnye zadachi sovremennogo estestvoznaniia* [The urgent tasks of contemporary natural science]. First pub. 1895, repub. as vol. 5 (1938) of Timiriazev, *Sochineniia* [Works]. 10 vols. (Moscow, 1937-40).

———. "Nauka" [Science]. In Russkii Bibliograficheskii Institut Granat, *Entsiklopedicheskii slovar'* [Encyclopedia Granat], 7th ed. (Moscow, n.d.), vol. 30, cols. 1-53.

———. *Nauka i demokratiia: Sbornik statei, 1904-1919 gg.* [Science and democracy: A collection of articles, 1904-1919]. Moscow, 1963.

———. "Probuzhdenie estestvoznaniia v tret'ei chetverti veka" [The awakening of natural science in the third quarter of the century]. In Russkii Bibliograficheskii Institut Granat, *Istoriia Rossii v XIX veke* [The Granat history of Russia in the 19th century], 9 vols. (St. Petersburg, 1907-11), 7: 1-30.

Timoshenko, Stephen P. *As I Remember: The Autobiography of Stephen P. Timoshenko.* Trans. by Robert Addis. Princeton, 1968.

———. "The Development of Engineering Education in Russia." *Russian Review* 15, no. 3 (1956): 173-85.

Ushinskii, K. D. *Izbrannye pedagogicheskie sochineniia* [Selected pedagogical works]. 2 vols. Moscow, 1953-54.

Valentinov, Aleksandr. *Poslednie studenty (Zapiski studenta)* [The last students: Notes of a student]. Berlin, 1922.

Valk, S. N., ed. *Sankt-Peterburgskie vysshie zhenskie (Bestuzhevskie) kursy, 1878-1918 gg.: Sbornik statei* [The St. Petersburg women's higher (Bestuzhev) courses, 1878-1918: Collection of articles]. Leningrad, 1965.

Vernadskii, G. V. "Bratstvo 'Priiutino'" [The Brotherhood of Shelter]. *Novyi Zhurnal* [New journal] 93 (1968): 147-71; 95 (1969): 202-15; 96 (1969): 153-71; 97 (1969): 218-37.

Vernadskii, Vladimir I. "The First Year of the Ukrainian Academy of Sciences (1918-1919)." *Annals of the Ukrainian Academy of Arts and Sciences in the U.S.* 11, no. 1-2 (31-32) (1964-68): 3-31.

———. *Ocherki i rechi* [Sketches and speeches]. 2 vols. Petrograd, 1922.

———. *Pis'ma o vysshem obrazovanii v Rossii* [Letters on higher education in Russia]. Moscow, 1913.

———. "1911 god v istorii russkoi umstvennoi kul'tury" [The year 1911 in the history of Russian intellectual culture]. In *Ezhegodnik gazety Rech' na 1912 god* [Yearbook of the newspaper *Rech'* for 1912], pp. 323-41. St. Petersburg, 1912.

———. "Vysshaia shkola i nauchnyia organizatsii" [The higher school and scientific organizations]. In *Ezhegodnik gazety Rech' na 1913 god* [Yearbook of the newspaper *Rech'* for 1913], pp. 351–71. St. Petersburg, 1913.

————. "Vysshaia shkola v Rossii" [The higher school in Russia]. In *Ezhegodnik gazety Rech' na 1914 god* [Yearbook of the newspaper *Rech'* for 1914], pp. 308–25. St. Petersburg, 1914.

Veselov, A. N. *Professional'no-tekhnicheskoe obrazovanie v SSSR: Ocherki po istorii srednego i nizshego proftekhobrazovaniia* [Vocational-technical education in the USSR: Studies in the history of secondary and primary vocational-technical education]. Moscow, 1961.

Vinogradov, P. G. "Uchebnoe delo v nashikh universitetakh" [The academic system in our universities]. *Vestnik Evropy* [Herald of Europe], 5 (October 1901), pp. 537–73.

Vucinich, Alexander. *Science in Russian Culture: A History to 1860.* Stanford, 1963. (Vucinich I.)

————. *Science in Russian Culture, 1861–1917.* Stanford, 1970. (Vucinich II.)

————. *Social Thought in Tsarist Russia: The Quest for a General Science of Society, 1861–1917.* Chicago, 1976.

*Vysshie zhenskie (Bestuzhevskie) kursy: Bibliograficheskii ukazatel'* [Women's higher (Bestuzhev) courses: Bibliographical guide]. Moscow, 1966.

Whittaker, Cynthia H. "The Women's Movement during the Reign of Alexander II: A Case Study in Russian Liberalism." *Journal of Modern History,* On-Demand Supplement, 48, no. 2 (June 1976): 35–69.

Woytinsky, W. S. *Stormy Passage: A Personal History through Two Russian Revolutions to Democracy and Freedom, 1905–1960.* New York, 1961.

Zaionchkovskii, P. A. *Rossiiskoe samoderzhavie v kontse XIX stoletiia* [The Russian autocracy at the end of the 19th century]. Moscow, 1970.

Zimmerman, Judith E. "Sociological Ideas in Pre-Revolutionary Russia." *Canadian-American Slavic Studies* 9 (Fall 1975): 302–23.

# INDEX